Home Buying

For

Smarties

The Consumer's Insider Guide

By Charles Chaplin
(no kidding)

**Binx
Publishing**

Seattle, WA

Published by Binx Publishing Seattle, WA

ISBN: 978-0-985210-3-2-8

Books by Charles Chaplin

Nonfiction

The Smarties Books: The Consumer's Insider Guides

Home Buying For Smarties

Home Selling For Smarties

Fiction

The Alex Campbell Real Estate Mystery Novel Series

No-List Alex (1)

No Serenity (2)

No Rest (3)

Note: these titles can be read in any order.

About This Book...

Whether you are a first time home buyer or a repeat home buyer, this book will organize your home buying venture and help you learn what to look out for and avoid! It is written from a consumer's standpoint by an experienced and active real estate agent who has been licensed since 1991. This book provides hands-on, agent-in-the-field information. There are real life stories and examples included which help to illustrate the information and points made.

Since 2004, I have volunteered to teach hundreds of free, certified home buying classes. The class is highly rated and everyone learns something, including me. Attendees kept telling me I should put the class information in a book. I listened and here it is! I share my opinions (good and bad) about the home buying process throughout. As I say at the start of each home buying class that I teach, some of what is mentioned will ring true with you and some of it will not. Take what you like and leave the rest; most important, think for yourself. But first, as with everything in business, here is the legal disclaimer. This will be a good trial run for you to read, as it certainly is a preview of what is to come when filling out purchase and sale paperwork!

The Not-so-Fine Print...

This book is intended for informational purposes only, to help home buyers become better informed and educated as to the home buying process before making a purchase. All information (factual or opinion) provided herein is from reliable sources but is not guaranteed. State residential real estate laws and practices vary. Legal terms, real estate terms, rules and regulations, common ways of doing business, may change or vary. It is up to the reader to independently investigate, verify and determine any changes and/or variations to the information provided herein. The "Real Life" sections and personal story examples have been altered to protect the identity of anyone involved.

This book is written from the standpoint of real estate regulations that are currently in place in Washington State, where the author practices. Other state laws and rules may vary. However, the overall information in this book should be helpful to any home buyer who is interested in purchasing within the United States. No legal, real estate, financial, or tax related advice is given or implied. The opinions expressed in this book are the author's and are based on his experience working in the industry and his unique take on the real estate industry. Readers should investigate any issues or opinions expressed in this book on their own and form their own conclusions. What is stated herein is not gospel and there are plenty of other opinions and approaches to consider when buying a home. Readers are encouraged to seek legal and other counsel as appropriate.

Note...

Throughout this book to keep things simple, I refer to a person who is selling real estate as a "real estate agent" or an "agent." There are varying title/role designations for different states. In some states, everyone licensed to sell real estate is referred to as a salesperson and in other states every licensee is referred to as a broker. The reader is encouraged to learn what the real estate licensee designations are in their state and what they mean. The forms that are referenced in this book are specific to Washington State, specifically to the Northwest Multiple Listing Service (NWMLS). These are the most common forms used by NWMLS members to list and sell properties. In some areas of Washington State, other MLS forms (not the NWMLS) are commonly used. Most states in the United States have different MLS systems that are commonly used by real estate agent members. The forms that are referenced in this book are a great jumping off point in terms of the reader learning more about the home buying process. The reader should easily be able to note the forms referenced or the business concept illustrated and find out how that applies in their own real estate market/state.

Okay, that hoop is jumped through, now on to the main event!

TABLE OF CONTENTS

ONE

GETTING ORGANIZED

I have sold everything from mobile homes to mansions and no matter what your price point, buying a home can be a stressful event. This is especially true if you are buying without a plan or real knowledge about the home buying process. Buying a house is probably the most expensive item you are ever going to purchase. The most important thing you can do to help yourself in the home buying process is to first assess your situation and get organized. This book is a great first step for doing just that!

Far too many people go about the home buying process with no real plan, buying on a whim, and working with people who do not have their true best interest at heart. It makes good sense to get organized and become informed about the home buying process ahead of time. By doing so, you will remove a lot of the innate drama and anxiety involved with buying a house. There are inherent risks in purchasing any kind of real estate and no one can completely guarantee anything. However, by getting organized up front and doing your homework, you will hopefully make a wiser decision to either buy or not buy.

Your Motivation...

The first question to ask when considering buying a house is, *"What is my motivation?"* Why am I thinking about doing this? Are you considering buying a place because: everyone says you should, your brother or coworker just bought a new home and you want to keep up, all of your friends are buying and you think you should too, your parents or children keep nagging you to buy a place, you hate your landlord, your rent just increased again, you have loud neighbors, you want to get a pet and your landlord won't allow pets, you are getting married, you are getting divorced, you are about to have children, you have a child and she needs a stable home, you just got a raise, a promotion, you got an inheritance, you won the lottery, you think investing money in real estate versus the stock market is a better long term investment, you want a yard, you want a shop or art studio, you are tired of paying rent to a landlord and not have that money go towards something you will eventually own, you can't bear the drab "landlord white" walls and want to control the décor, on and on…, whew!

There are many questions to ask and consider. You will catch on real fast that I am a big proponent of answering these questions, getting facts, and becoming informed <u>before</u> you start ambling around and looking at open houses like a boat without a rudder.

Timeline…

Assuming you answered some of the motivational questions above and you are still thinking about buying a place, the next thing to ponder is your timeline. Many people have asked me over the years, "*When is the best time to buy?*" Short and sweet, there really is no "best" time to buy. Rather it is what best suits your unique situation. One of the biggest changes I have seen in my years of selling residential real estate is that in my market/region it used to be that you could count on July and August being very slow and from about Thanksgiving to mid

January was another dead season. That is no longer the case, sales now happen year round. I have literally sold houses on Christmas day. I attribute some of this change to the explosion of the internet and the ability for the public to peruse listings when it best suits them; i.e. while bored stiff after Aunt Agnes' burned Thanksgiving dinner. Sure, some time periods are busier than others but real estate is now a yearlong venture. Different regions of the country have different slow and busy real estate seasons. Contrary to what many think, in the Seattle area the sunny summer months tend to be slower for residential sales. My theory is we are so sun deprived, that everyone is outside enjoying the sun while we have it. But there are still summer sales; in fact the fourth of July has usually been a sales day for me, go figure! I would advise not getting too hung up on the fast and slow seasons for your region, maybe be aware of them but keep in mind your own unique situation and timeline and work from there.

What kind of lease do you currently have, is it month-to-month, yearly? How many days in advance do you have to provide written notice to your landlord that you are moving? You and the real estate agent you choose to work with will want to review this right off the bat so that you can hopefully time your purchase and closing with your lease's expiration. What is your approximate timeline if you move forward with purchasing? Do you want to purchase something in the next few months or is it urgent and your landlord is tearing down your building and you have 30 days to vacate! If you currently own and are considering selling and buying a new place, organizing your new home search and the sale of your current property is crucial. You will benefit from the buying tips in this book.

The Pros of Buying...

It is always good to do a simple review of the pros of buying versus renting first, before you rush out and start looking. This list is not comprehensive and you may have some items to add. The main thing is that you think about the pros of each scenario in advance.

When you buy, the typical advantages (pros) are:

1. You build equity
2. You have more stability
3. There could be a tax advantage
4. Pets might be possible
5. You have more control over the décor and how things are maintained or not.

Equity (the value of a piece of property over and above any mortgage or other liens relating to it) is a term used to describe the gain or positive value in a property. For example, you purchase a place for $200,000 and live there for five to seven years, which is the general rule of thumb timeframe most home purchasers need to abide by in order to sell their place and break even or hopefully make a profit, gain equity. Let's say you purchase a condominium (condo) for $200,000 and six years later you sell it for $230,000. The $30,000 is your equity in that property, the amount you gain less the sales fees and taxes. Equity is great, right? It's great when it works. But economists have a term "negative equity" which they use to politely describe when you are losing money. So you purchase for $200,000 and you have to sell a year later. The market has dropped and now you are selling for $180,000. Thus you are losing $20,000 plus your sales fees and taxes. You have negative equity in the property. Not a preferred scenario and certainly something we have all heard about in recent years with the national real estate market crash.

This is why I always advise clients to make sure they can see themselves living in the property they are buying for at least five to seven years, maybe longer depending on the real estate cycle and your local market conditions. If you could get transferred in a year or you are single and think you might get married in the next few years and will want to unload your bachelor pad, then you need to put some thought into this. If you get transferred or married or just decide you want to move in a year or so, no one can guarantee what the real estate market will be doing. If you are lucky, the market might be in a boom phase and you will make a nice profit. Or you may lose money and in that case are you prepared for that or would it be possible to rent out your place if you have to leave? If you own a condominium or co-op, the rental option will depend on the rules and regulations of your home owner association. If it is feasible to rent, do you want to become a landlord? Are you prepared to hire a property management company to handle your rental property? Lots of issues to sort out and it is best to think about these now, before you buy something.

Next on the home buying advantage list is stability. When you own a property there is more stability, literally and psychologically. Literally because hopefully you will secure a stable 20 or 30 year fixed rate mortgage and you will have a spreadsheet that shows what your monthly payments will be for the next 20 or 30 years. You may wonder if you are even going to still be alive when the last payment due date outlined on that huge payment spreadsheet occurs! Anyway, there is your monthly mortgage payment schedule in black and white.

Of course, as the years pass, there will be tax increases and home owner dues increases (if applicable) but the base mortgage or "rent" is the same. No more Ms. Landlord randomly increasing your rent or telling you that you need to vacate because her sister is going to be moving to your town and needs to live in your apartment. There is also psychological stability when you buy. This is the sense of control in knowing you now own, you have a piece of land, a stake in the local neighborhood/community. When you own, you may want to put down roots, get to know your neighbors better, become involved in community events. You have a greater sense of belonging via the stability of owning. Also, for better or worse, when you own you have more stability or control over maintaining the property. The leaky faucet, the broken closet door, you get to decide if and when those items are repaired. No more sitting around and waiting two years for the landlord to take care of them.

Third on our list is the possible tax advantage that no doubt everyone and their cousin Mimi have told you about. It may very well be that buying a property is indeed a tax advantage for you. But the only qualified person to address this issue is a certified tax preparer, tax accountant or tax lawyer. Someone who is qualified/trained to look at your annual tax returns, your bank account and investments and say, "*yes*" or "*no*," buying a home is to your advantage come tax time. Your real estate agent, your loan person, hair stylist, cousin, best friend are not qualified to answer this question. Go to someone who is qualified and verify it with them.

Here is a **tip**. Always go to the appropriate source to get questions answered and you will have a better outcome. If you have questions about your mortgage payment, talk to your loan person. If you are curious about the current state of the real estate market then talk to a real estate agent not your hair stylist. I cannot tell you the number of times I have heard, "*Well my hair stylist says the market is picking up and my home's value has increased by at least 20%.*" Really? I did not know beauty school included a license to practice real estate. Get the picture? You might be amazed at the number of seemingly very intelligent people who do not follow this tip and do not go to the appropriate source for the best information/result. As a side note, many people believe whatever they find on the internet as gospel. This has led some to think because they research a property value using a common internet search, they are then in the know and have an accurate picture of the market and values. That could not be more misguided. The property values you can find online are helpful but they are most often off from the current reality of what is actually taking place in the market. This is where having an agent who is active and out in the field comes in handy. Their sense of the market combined with comparative analysis provides a much more accurate picture of current market conditions and values.

Next up is pets. Sometimes landlords can be very strict about no pets when you rent. If you have pets illegally where you are renting, then you know firsthand the stress this causes when the landlord stops by for a visit; i.e. hiding Fluffy the cat in the closet, putting bunny in the laundry hamper! So maybe a big reason you are buying is you want to get the dog you have always wanted or another cat, a bunny, chickens, a python, an iguana, a tarantula, a squirrel and even a cow (I'm not kidding story to follow). In my opinion, a good real estate agent is going to want to know about any current pets you have or if you intend to get pets. Your agent should ask about this before you start looking for properties. This is true even if you are purchasing a single family, residential, ranch style house with a fenced back yard. Some single family residential neighborhoods have restrictions on pets just like condos. You need to let your agent know that you have a 27 pound dog, a 10 pound cat, hamsters, even a goldfish. Yes, there really are condo complexes that forbid having a goldfish, probably even a pet rock. Hopefully your real estate agent will ask you about pets when you first meet. I could write pages about those that do not ask and the horrific outcomes that follow.

Make sure your agent also knows if you currently do not have a pet but when you purchase, you intend to get the Labrador Retriever you have always wanted. If you have pets and your real estate agent is smart, he will try to ensure that any condo complex you look at allows pets. More important if they do, he will ask ahead of time what the current weight/breed restrictions are in that complex. Nothing is worse than to find a condo you like and are excited to make an offer on, only to discover that dogs over 20 pounds are not allowed and the Labrador you intend to get weighs 60 pounds. Even worse is if you purchase such a place and move in only to have the condo management inform you that your Labrador is not allowed to live there. An organized agent will most likely write your current pets (breeds, weights) into your purchase and sale agreement so everyone is informed ahead of time of your current pet situation. However, it is still up to you the buyer to read all the condominium rules and regulations and verify firsthand that your pet is allowed. If you are going to get a pet once you move in, your agent could write that into the purchase and sale agreement as well, *"Buyer will have one Labrador Retriever, approximately sixty (60) pounds, living in her unit."* Something like that.

The last item on our buying advantage list is décor. When you own, if you want to make the place a Jefferson Airplane psychedelic flashback pad, paint the living room walls bright purple with an orange ceiling and lime green floors, knock yourself out. The color wheel is your only limitation! Try this when you rent and see what your landlord thinks when he drops by. It is called not getting your security deposit back. Landlords are partial to their white or beige walls which you may have discovered can be very drab and depressing after a while. When you own, you can go wild with the décor if you choose. Just keep in mind, if you purchase a condo or townhome there most likely will be rules about what you can and cannot do on your balcony, patio area. Also in a condo, any structural changes you may intend to make will need written board approval first. Notice I said "written" not verbal. I could write stories about that point for hours. If you want to replace the carpeting with hardwood floors, or you want to knock out the small divider (non-supporting) wall between the kitchen and living room, apply for permission and get written permission from your condo's board first. Your condo board may even require permission if you are simply changing out the appliances. It bears repeating, get written permission from your condo board first before you undertake any remodeling project in your unit. Typically painting your interior walls is not something they require permission for, but you never know so check your condo rules and regulations first.

Over the years I have seen many a situation where a condo owner illegally installed hardwood floors or made structural changes without first obtaining written permission from the condo home owner association/board. Some of these folks got caught making their unapproved changes while the work was being done and were forced to stop the work. Others were found out years later when they listed their condo for sale and the association/board then discovered the illegal changes. In some cases, the homeowner's association forced the owner to change things back such that they were legal before selling the unit; i.e. ripping out the unapproved hardwood floors. Not a pleasant situation. So, keep it simple and always get written approval from the association/board before you make any major interior changes in your condo. Some condo complexes are loose and anything goes and others are like lock down in Stalingrad. We'll talk more about condos later. Also, if you purchase a single family residential property there may be neighborhood covenants that prohibit you from having a red front door or you can only paint the exterior one of the approved colors.

The Pros of Renting…

Those were some of the pros of buying, now for the pros of renting. The main advantages of renting include:

1. Greater mobility
2. Repair work
3. Less expensive (sometimes).

When you rent, mobility is always an advantage. Do you have neighbors that keep waking you up at 2:00 a.m. or a perhaps a baby elephant lives above you and her stomping around keeps you up at night? It is way easier to get out of your lease and move to a quieter place than if you own this noisy unit. If you are renting and you get a great job promotion offer that requires a transfer to Toledo, then you get out of your lease and move on. When you own however, you have to then figure out if you can afford to sell your unit right now and move to Toledo. Or can you rent the unit; does the association allow rentals? Can you afford to rent your unit at a price that covers your mortgage and home owner dues, property management fees? If not, you might be stuck and not relocating for your job promotion in Toledo. No one knows the future but food for thought if you are in a field or on a career path that involves frequent relocating in order to progress.

Advantage two when you rent is repair work. When the pipes break in the middle of the night, you are not thrilled but in theory that repair is on your landlord's dime (actually tens of thousands of dimes). Maintaining the apartment's roof, parking lot, garbage, windows, etc…, are all items your landlord is hopefully doing. When you own, those items will be your rainy day headache, especially if you are purchasing a single family home but even if you are purchasing a condo your monthly dues go toward maintaining those items.

One final advantage of renting is that in certain real estate cycles it is sometimes less expensive in the short run to rent than to buy. This is not always true. It depends where we are in the real estate cycle and what the interest rates for mortgages are currently doing. But if it is cheaper to buy than to rent, you will want to think that through first. Typically, if you are currently renting a two bedroom unit or your rental comes with a killer balcony or a premium parking space, when you go to buy you may not get those perks. Especially if you only want to buy in the same neighborhood you are currently renting in and you only want to pay your current monthly rent amount or less for a monthly mortgage payment.

For example, right now you rent a two bedroom apartment with a great parking space for $1,000 a month and you only want to purchase within your immediate neighborhood, nothing else will do. You do not want your monthly mortgage and home owner expenses to exceed your current rent of $1,000. Not always, but quite frequently, this will mean you will only be able to afford to purchase a one bedroom unit or you can afford a two bedroom unit but it does not come with parking like your rental unit has. You have to step down (lose one of your rental benefits like the extra room or parking) to buy and keep your current $1,000 a month housing payment. You will want to explore this first and ask yourself, can I live in a one bedroom, and will my life be miserable without the premium parking space? Can

I expand my bubble and look at other neighborhoods that I have not considered? Is there another neighborhood where my $1,000 monthly payment can get me a place that is similar to or better than what I am currently renting?

House Rich and Life Poor...

The last thing I always add when you are figuring out your motivation and timeline, and the pros of buying versus renting is, *Do Not End Up House Rich and Life Poor.* Repeat that phrase; in fact make it your mantra, *Do Not End Up House Rich and Life Poor.* By this I mean you intend to only spend $200,000 and that is what your budget shows is best. But you go out and start looking and before you know it you are purchasing a place for $275,000. To do this, you are going to wait tables on the weekends in addition to your full time weekly job. Or you are going to purchase the $275,000 place and that means you will no longer go away on vacation, no more nights out, sports events, etc.... Is it really worth it to cut out all the fun things in your life in order to keep a roof over your head? It is easy to get swayed and lose all reason when you are buying a house. Suddenly purchasing this $275,000 dream place is worth more to you than having a life. You are then in danger of becoming *House Rich and Life Poor.* You have a great house and no life because all of your time and money are going to pay for the house.

Think twice about this, actually think more than twice. This is why choosing a team to truly represent you and your best interest is of the utmost importance. It is very easy for your emotions to be swayed and for you to get carried away when making this expensive purchase.

If you are working with an unethical real estate agent or loan person, they are not going to give you a time out for a reality check. They will be there blowing more smoke and encouraging you to push your limits to buy this dream place. You need to think twice about getting into something more expensive than you originally intended. It is easy for sales people to push you to spend more and stretch your budget because they aren't going to be the ones actually living in and paying for the house. This is why the next chapter is all about choosing the right real estate agent and loan person. Putting together a team you can trust. You want to make an informed and well thought out decision about these key players in advance before you are swept away in the built-in wave of emotions and drama that inevitably comes with buying a property.

Snooze and Lose...

Some might ask, "*Why do all this prep work ahead of time when I can just look online myself? I can visit open houses and when I find what I like call an agent and lender to help me.*" That is a valid question and there is some online work you can do now. I find my buyers are way more tuned in and up on the market now than ever before thanks to the internet explosion. This is good, as it cuts down the reality of the market lesson I used to have to do with clients. Looking at listings online while you are getting organized is probably a good idea and most do it. However, I would strongly suggest you get organized and put together a team to help you at the start of your search not when you have found your dream place to buy online and are ants-in-the-pants ready to buy. Here is why I say this. Far too many times I have gotten new clients who have gone through this fire drill before contacting me. So they have looked online and maybe dropped in on open houses and suddenly they have found the place they want to buy. They have done no real prep work, are not pre-approved for a loan, so they really do not have an accurate idea as to what they can afford and they are fairly clueless about the home buying process. They frantically call me and say they have found their dream home and they want to write up an offer right away. Or they are a bit calmer and ask me what they need to do in order to write up an offer.

I then meet with them and go through the hour long intake appointment, review all the materials and they figure out pretty fast, there is more work to putting together an offer than they imagined. In today's market, no seller is going to seriously consider an offer from a buyer who is not pre-approved or cannot provide them with a funds availability letter if they buying with cash. It is a waste of the seller's time and they do not want to be bothered. So the loan pre-approval has to be taken care of and this takes time. Typically what happens is the dream house they are so excited about sells before they can get their act together to write up a valid offer. Or by the time they contact me, the place they are so excited about has already gone pending inspection (sold).

A while back, a friend of mine's co-worker casually asked me to help her once she was ready to buy a condo. I explained to her how I work; we needed to meet and review things and she needed to go get pre-approved for a loan first. I even gave her my recommended lender list so she could start the process. I did not hear back from her for a couple of months. Then one Sunday afternoon out of the blue, she frantically called me. She found a condo she wanted to buy. What did she need to do? I asked if she had followed through and found a lender and gotten pre-approved yet. No, she had been too busy. So she went first thing Monday morning and visited lenders and started the process of getting pre-approved. The condo she was excited about was a great place and had just listed the previous Friday. By Monday afternoon it was pending inspection, essentially sold if all went well. This woman was a day late and dollar short. Because she procrastinated, she ended up missing out. Had she followed through when I originally spoke with her, I could have set up her search and been sending her listings. I would have sent her the condo listing on Friday right when it listed and conceivably since she was organized and ready, we could have seen the place on Friday, written up an offer on Friday and beat the offer that was submitted and accepted on Sunday. This happens far too often. So hopefully it shows you why I think getting organized and having an agent help you from the very start is in your best interest.

Real Life...

Here's the story I promised. A few years back I was doing my intake meeting with a new buyer client. When she got to my form's blank about pets and she wrote in "*cow*." I laughed and thought she was kidding me. No. She had researched cows, and had already picked out the Holstein cow she intended to have live in her new back yard. She wasn't buying in a condo complex so what was the problem? For starters, the city zoning regulations, the neighborhood covenants.

16

Long story short, I crossed off her in-city neighborhood choice and eventually I found her a great house outside of the city in an area that does not have restrictions on having a cow in the backyard. She now lives outside of the city with her cow, Daisy, and life is good. I visited and Daisy is sweet, although the glass of fresh milk from Daisy that I was offered is another story. Anyway, we communicated before she started touring properties and my client and her cow are legal and happy. Imagine if we hadn't spoken about any prospective pets she intended to have and she purchased a house in the city as she originally planned. At a minimum, there would have been a lot of disappointment when the city and/or neighbors told her Daisy the cow had to go.

Hopefully, you are beginning to see the method to my madness and the importance of working with a real estate agent who is organized and encourages you to plan ahead and effectively communicate your needs.

TWO

CHOOSING YOUR TEAM

A ssuming you made it through chapter one, you have weighed the pros of buying versus the pros of renting specific to your situation and you have decided to proceed with buying a property. The next step is to put together your team. Your team consists of the people you are going to interview and choose to represent you in your transaction. Very similar to if you are an employer and you are hiring a new employee.

Choosing Your Real Estate Agent...

Sometimes class attendees will ask me why they should have a buyer's agent represent them. My response to them is, *"Would you represent yourself in a court of law?"* If not, then why would you make the most expensive purchase of your life without having someone (hopefully experienced and ethical) represent you from the start to the finish? The next thing I typically hear after my response is, *"I don't want to have to pay an agent."* Well guess what, the buyer usually never pays their agent to represent them. How does this work, how does the buyer's agent get paid? The seller lists a house for sale and part of the stated commission is paid to your real estate agent's brokerage. The brokerage then deducts their assorted fees (sometimes quite hefty) and then issues a commission check to your real estate agent. There are other business models where you the buyer pay the brokerage that is representing you for each step of the process as you go. Some of these types of brokerages may state they will refund the cash you paid to them once the commission from the sale is paid or they will refund you at closing. Some of these plans are legitimate and others appear to be operating in a legal gray zone (that's polite for breaking the law). It is up to you to use your best judgment and determine what type of brokerage service works best for you. Explore options but the type of representation I will refer to in this book is what a traditional full service/full time agent does. This type of service means that you the buyer pay nothing to your agent's brokerage or your agent to represent you. With this type of service model, your real estate agent is with you from the very beginning, through the offer process, the inspection(s), escrow, and your closing. They will probably follow up with you for years because they want to list your place 10 years later when you are ready to sell. The full service agent is your point of contact; you are not handed off to different people as the transaction progresses. In my opinion, this keeps things much more orderly, there is a lower margin for error with one person in charge, and the result is less anxiety and confusion for you.

How do you find a full service real estate agent to work with? Naturally you can search online, jot down agent names that are plastered on the bus stop benches and grocery carts, ask friends and family who they worked with, talk to your second cousin Bill who just got his real estate license, etc…. I would first like to remind you again that this is likely the most expensive item you will purchase in your lifetime or it will rank right up there. It is not like you are buying a sweater and you take it home and decide it doesn't look good on you and return it two weeks later. This is why doing your research and getting organized ahead of time will allow you to hopefully find something that truly suits your needs.

No Friends or Family...

I personally do not work with someone I am related to or am close friends with. Here's why. Let's say you are an agent and your sister is moving to town. Simple, she will buy something and you will be her agent right? No! There might be all sorts of unresolved sibling rivalry issues still at play. Subconsciously you might look at listings and delete those that are better than what you own; you don't want your sister getting something better than what you have. You most likely will make assumptions that you should not, "*I know my sister won't like this listing; this is not right for her.*" Based on what, the tastes you recall she had when you were growing up? There is too much history and family baggage to clutter your thinking. You won't be as objective or neutral, as an unrelated agent will be. Also, what if you are your sister's agent and you make a huge mistake or screw something up with her deal? Say she misses out on the house of her dreams and rightly or wrongly she holds you (her agent) responsible. Thanksgivings spent together are going to be real fun with her sitting there resenting you for making her miss out on her dream house. It may not even be true that you the agent did anything to hamper her deal and cause her to miss out on her dream place but the perception of that is still there. In my opinion, having a family member act as your agent and buying a house usually do not mix well together.

Next, there is your best friend Stephanie who is a long time licensed real estate agent. She is all gung-ho to help you buy a place. I always caution that the same problems with a family member might happen with a friend. Also, your friend working as your real estate agent might not be on her toes as much as she would be with a neutral client. There is a good chance that agent Stephanie will be a bit more lax, "*Oh, I'm 40 minutes late but Carl won't mind because we are friends and he knows I'm always running late.*" Or, "*Legally I need Carl to fill this form out tonight but we are friends and I know he won't sue me so we'll just do it later.*" The professional boundaries get blurred; the agent is not as alert. If you become annoyed with the job your friend (agent Stephanie) is doing and you want to switch to another agent, how awkward is that going to be? It could put a real damper on your friendship. So why bother, don't go there.

Contrary to what you may think or have heard, pick someone who is professional, has a good track record, with whom you click, but who is not related to you or a good friend. It keeps things simple. There is enough inherent drama and emotion involved in buying a house; you don't need to add family and friendship baggage to the mix! If you are pressured by others to use family or friend to represent you, tell them it is nothing personal, just business. You like to keep your business affairs separate from your personal life. If their egos can't handle that response, then that is their problem to work out. There is too much money involved in purchasing a house for this process not to be a business venture and treated accordingly.

Another point to make on this topic of family and friends is if they represent you, then they are going to know all of your business, literally. They will know what you can and cannot afford. If you are buying with a spouse or partner, they will see up close and personal how you two interact. Suddenly your world of friends and family knows all of your personal business. *"She can't afford a house on the bluffs. He's a rude jerk when he tours. She really is a picky princess. They are indecisive. They fight like cats and dogs, is their marriage on the rocks?"* Even if you work with a friend or family member who does not gossip, sometimes things slip out by accident. If you choose team members who are outside of your family and friend sphere, neutral and competent professionals, then your personal business should stay where it belongs, in the vault! If you pick a person who is outside of your sphere who is an enormous gossip (and legally they shouldn't be gabbing about you), who are they going to gossip with, their dog? They don't know your friends and family and so your personal information remains private.

The Referral...

Then there is the referral. Let's say your sister or coworker has a real estate agent or loan officer that they think is absolutely wonderful. That is good to know, take it into consideration. However, do not go on auto pilot and think, *"My search is over, I'll just work with Bob because Suzie says Bob is the best."* Suzie may very well be correct and this loan person or agent Bob is the best. But you still should do your own vetting and make sure you agree with Suzie's strong recommendation. You might be surprised to learn that Suzie gets a referral fee (legal in some states and illegal in others) from this awesome agent named Bob for referring you to him. You may discover Suzie is naive and this agent or loan person is a terrific manipulator, well versed in stroking egos (more about manipulators later). Just make sure you personally investigate those who are referred to you and that they meet your criteria of what you are looking for. Do not assume that since X referred this agent or loan person to me then they must be fine and that's all I need to know or do. Doing that would be working on auto pilot and it can (and usually does) come back to bite you.

No Newbie's, Retirees, Dilettantes, Part-timers…

I would personally avoid a new real estate agent or a new loan officer. Clearly, everyone has to start somewhere and get established but it would be far better for you to have an experienced team, who has been around the race track and in the trenches a few hundred times or more. A newbie might be nice, diligent, and ethical but their lack of hands-on experience can backfire. There are ways for a newbie to build their career. They could start out as a licensed agent's assistant or work the processing end of lending or they could pair up for a year or so with a seasoned agent or mentor who is hands-on involved with each step of their transactions to ensure things are not overlooked. Meaning, the new agent trails the experienced agent and acts essentially as their gopher, learns the business side by side. Beware the new agent who says all is good because his office manager or the designated broker will be personally reviewing all his paperwork. They do that for all agents regardless of their experience level and years in the business. In my opinion, the hands-on help is needed out in the field and when writing up your offer and negotiating, not after the fact. A newbie in this field who say previously sold cars or skin care products, or recently earned their MBA is not really up to speed in my opinion. This does not mean the newbie is not well intentioned or intelligent. They just do not have (in my opinion) the practical, hands-on and intuitive experience that is necessary and crucial to ensure your home buying experience is as easy as it can be.

The real estate industry has a history of taking on anyone who has done the cursory training for a license. Unfortunately, the industry joke has long been, *"If you can breathe on a mirror and you like people then you are in business. Go out there and fly by the seat of your pants, fake it until you make it or fail."* Most do not succeed big surprise. This is part of the reason why real estate is such a high turnover industry. And the in-house training that brokerages used to require for new agents continues to diminish as this industry changes. Not that a majority of that kind of education was ever very helpful. I personally found it to be little more than a glorified charm school; i.e. learn to dress for success, corporate rah-rah, and manipulation skills 101.

Next, there is the retired grandma and dilettante real estate agent. These are typically well meaning individuals who are retired and/or independently wealthy. They are looking for a little diversion or an identity to make their life a bit more interesting, so they decide to sell real estate. In my experience, these can be some of the worst agents out there. They are not really motivated to stay on top of the constantly changing rules, forms, and laws that this industry is known for. These agents tend to putter about and make a sale in between their holiday trips, their social club events, and their winters in Palm Springs. They are pretty much playing real estate agent to keep themselves occupied. I would advise finding an agent who is working this business full time, who is out there making deals, committed first to their work, not their leisure life. That said, you do not have to hire a Type A nut bucket either, a balance is nice. A super busy agent will not have as much time to spend with you. As a side note, just because someone is a senior citizen and looks like Mr. or Mrs. Santa Claus, does not mean that they are ethical or competent. Please do not go on auto pilot because someone's looks conjures up warm and fuzzy, childhood story book images for you or they are so model perfect and sexy that you overlook the fact that they are dumber than a post. Hang out with Mr. and Mrs. Claus at bingo night or stop by Hooters or Chippendale's if you want to ogle flesh.

Finally, there are the part-timer agents, my least favorite. These people have full time jobs/careers and think they can make big bucks on the side by selling real estate to all their family, friends, and co-workers. Contrary to what many may say or believe, I do not think selling real estate is a part time job. To do this job effectively and provide a client with the best level of service, I think your agent needs to be a full time, full service agent. I cringe whenever I call a listing agent, only to be connected to their voice mail at their full time job at one of the local corporations or governmental agencies; don't these big entities have anti moonlighting clauses in their employee contracts? When something crucial regarding the transaction is needed in the middle of the workday, where are these charming part time agents? In a staff meeting at their real job! In my experience, these folks rarely are on top of real estate laws, inventory, or the correct way of doing business. How could they be? They already have a full time job. Previewing houses for their buyer client online while working at their full time job is not old school, in-person previewing. Online previewing does not give an agent a true understanding of the inventory or the current state of the market. Nor is Ms. Part-timer who is trying to postpone a buyer's inspection appointment to suit her full time work schedule's time constraints very consumer friendly either. Usually the full time, full service agent involved in a deal with a part time agent has to essentially take over the deal and work both ends of it to make it come together and happen. The part time agent still ends up with their portion of the commission though. The part time agent might fake it and put the work off on the other full time agents, but eventually I have observed these part time agents usually lose their license for incompetence or negligence or their clients begin to figure out part time means less for them and quit using them. These agents typically go out of business. Or they pick up the clue phone and start working this job full time and providing the level of full time service that their clients deserve and the legalities of this business demands.

I think there is one possible exception for a part time agent. If the agent lives in a rural location, say a remote town of 3,000 residents or less, or they are on a small vacation island, then unless they are independently wealthy they probably will need to have another full time job in order to survive. Real estate is truly part time where they live as there is not much inventory to cover, not many transactions happening, and way less to keep up on. In my opinion, any agent who is good and working in a metro area should be able to sell real estate full time and offer full time, full service to their clients. Again, buying or selling your home is probably the most expensive thing you will do, why have a part-timer represent you?

Interviewing Agents...

When you have your short list of real estate agents to interview, try to get a sense when you meet with a prospective agent of how he works. Is their personality a good match for yours? Do they know what they are doing or are they all charm and no substance? What is their intake packet like? Is it informative and educational or just pre-made corporate bunk their company provides with glossy stock image photos and not much substance? Do they have a pre-made iPad or laptop company video and try and wow you with bells and whistles? Have they gone completely Hollywood and instead of meeting with you, they email you a video about themselves and their company? Technology can be useful but in this game, hands-on information that actually educates and true competence is crucial. It is great if your real estate agent has a good personality and you enjoy their company. However, the most important part is if they are informative, competent, ethical, timely and organized. When it comes down to the purchase and sale forms, the offer timelines, negotiation, can they deliver? A **tip**, just because an agent is a "top producer" or well known, does not automatically mean they are ethical or good, especially from a consumer standpoint.

Questions to Ask an Agent...

Here is a list of questions you may want to ask a real estate agent when you interview them. After the list is more detailed information on each question's topic. I hope this list helps fire up your brain. You may have questions of your own to add based on your specific situation and needs.

1. How many years have you been working as an active and licensed real estate agent?

2. What do these titles, designations, abbreviations, listed on your business card mean?

3. Are you a member of NAR?

4. Do you specialize in working with buyers?

5. Do you do dual agency?

6. Are you a full time, full service agent? Will I be working directly with you from the start of my search until the end?

7. Do you think it is always necessary for a buyer to pay for an inspection on the property he is buying?

8. How do you pre-qualify properties before I tour them?

9. How many clients are you currently working with and what is your client limit?

10. What is your opinion of working with two buyers with the same criteria and price range?

11. What are your thoughts about a Buyer Agency Agreement?

12. On the Financing Addendum, where do you get the necessary information to fill in when we write up an offer?

13. Before I go on a house tour with you, do I need to be pre-approved for a loan or have my funds availability letter?

14. What are some typical out-of-pocket expenses that I need to know about for the home buying process?

15. Did you write the information contained in your intake packet?

16. What sort of references can you provide?

17. Do you specialize in a particular neighborhood or area?

18. Have you ever been sued by a former client or disciplined by any real estate professional organization? (i.e. the local MLS, board of Realtors, state licensing board)

19. Have you ever been convicted of a crime or been incarcerated?

20. What is your level of education?

Question One: You want to know how long they have been selling real estate. Did they just get their license? Do they sell real estate full time? How long have they sold real estate in your state? Are they up on the laws/business norms in your state?

Question Two: Ask them to explain what their title or designations on their business card mean. Some titles and designations are less impressive than you might imagine (bordering on made up). I won't pick on any specific ones here but use your common sense. You can also research these titles and designations online as well. If you read the "Note" at the start of this book, you know I am generically referring to anyone who is licensed to sell real estate as either an agent or real estate agent. Different states have different terms. In Washington State, everyone who has a real estate license is now referred to as a Broker. Then there is a Managing Broker level, which in Washington State means they have been an active real estate licensee for three years and worked full time as an agent, have taken additional training, passed more tests, and they can legally open and operate their own real estate brokerage and/or manage other brokers in the office. Finally there is the Designated Broker who is the person appointed to run the real estate office, through whom disputes are ultimately mediated. There is the Owner (sometimes they also act as the Designated Broker) and they own the brokerage. You may want to find out what the titles are and how they work in your state. As you can see, being called a "real estate broker" in Washington State is not something to be impressed with. It just means the person has a basic license to sell real estate.

Question Three: NAR is the National Association of Realtors. What do you the consumer care about this? Well, if an agent pays annual dues and is a member of NAR, then there is another level of protection should things go wrong. If you have serious problems with your agent and she is a Realtor, then you can report her to NAR and file a complaint against her behavior with them. The regional branch of NAR will most likely intervene and look into to your grievances. Conceivably, if your agent is really bad, then NAR might kick her out for her unethical behavior. So there is some extra assurance if your agent is a member of NAR (a Realtor) that they must uphold the NAR Code of Ethics and be more accountable. You can Google this topic and visit the NAR website if you want to learn more.

To add a bit of confusion to this, there is the term Realtor. That is a trademarked word, coined and owned by the National Association of Realtors. Pronounced "real" and "tor" there is no "i" in the spelling or correct pronunciation; i.e. "*Realitor*" or "*Realiter*" is incorrect. Those who are not dues paying members of NAR are not permitted to use the word Realtor or the Realtor logo.

Question Four: Is this agent someone who is well versed with representing and helping buyers? The old school norm is that most agents pursued listings because it was seen as less work. That may or may not be true. But your agent needs to be experienced with the buyer side of deals and be well versed in the educational, touring and organizational prep work that is involved on the buyer end. Do they volunteer to teach home buyer classes, do they mostly work as a buyer's agent, etc…? Show me your track record, do not just tell me. Also, just because someone has a designation that proclaims they are a buyer's representative does not necessarily tell you very much. It means they took a clock hour class (all agents have to accrue educational clock hours to keep their licenses active). They can now use that title proclaiming they represent buyers. Not a bad thing in and of itself but it does not show you how much they have actively spent representing buyers.

Question Five: I hope they answer no! Dual agency is not legal in some states but currently it is legal in Washington State. Dual agency means your real estate agent is representing you the buyer and the seller in the transaction. They are going to keep their mouth shut and neutrally represent both parties and incidentally they are going to collect a double commission for working both sides of the transaction. I have never understood ethically how this works. In my opinion, no one can remain neutral when they are representing both sides of a deal. At a minimum there is body language, word slips, tone of voice, etc.... For me, dual agency has always been analogous to an attorney representing both the plaintiff and the defendant. How would that work to either party's advantage except the agent's bank account? I have never done a dual agency deal because I do not think they are fair to either the buyer or the seller. Quite a few agents, some very successful, do act as a dual agents. I would suggest you the client not agree to that. The purchase and sale agreement (in WA State) has boxes where the agent indicates who they are representing.

Here is a **tip** about dual agency. When you drive around and see big time agent X's for sale signs, note when you see one of his yard signs and on top of it is a sold sign rider with his name on it too. Most likely, this agent is proudly letting you know that he represented both the seller and buyer in this purchase. You can see via the signs that some tout this as a great thing; great for who?

In my case, since I do not do dual agency, if I take a listing (let's say it is a two bedroom townhouse in the south end listed for $285,000) and one of my buyers is looking at properties that this listing's criteria falls under (i.e. two bedroom townhouse in the south end priced $300,000 and below). I immediately notify my buyer that I have taken this listing. If they have interest in seeing it, I refer them to another real estate agent to work with for this specific listing only. If they tour my seller's listing and decide to make an offer, then the other agent represents them. If they do not have an interest in my listing, then we continue to work together and look at other listings that are not mine. This keeps things real simple, fair, and it's not difficult to work this way.

One point to note, if your agent has a listing that you are interested in, she is representing the sellers as the listing agent, she may refer you to another agent who works in her brokerage. For example, your agent hangs her license with XYZ Realty that is her brokerage. She does not do dual agency so she refers you to Amy who also hangs her license with XYZ Realty, the same brokerage. Technically, XYZ Realty is the brokerage for both of these agents and if one of their agents represents the buyer in the sale of one of their other agent's listings, one could also call this dual agency. The brokerage, XYZ Realty, has an agent representing a seller and another agent, Amy, representing a buyer for one of their brokerage's listings. That too is commonly referred to as dual agency. My point for you is that the same agent does not represent both the buyer and the seller in a single transaction. As long as there are two different agents, one representing the seller and one representing the buyer in a transaction, I do not see a conflict of interest or problem with both of the agents having their licenses hanging in the same brokerage, XYZ Realty. The agents are not (should not) be colluding behind the scenes regardless if they are from the same brokerage or two completely different brokerages.

Question Six: We touched on the full service agent topic a few pages back. This is the traditional, one person going through the entire deal with you, helping you, being accountable, etc.... I am partial to this method because I think the buyer is better served not being passed off to different people in various stages of their deal. I do not think buyers need to be paying certain fees for agent representation, regardless if it is refunded at the end or not. The refund part can trigger issues with the loan end of things. Any money that is coming back to you, being paid to you either before a deal closes or after, needs to be reported to your loan person. They legally have to take into account this money and it could potentially screw up your loan/income ratio. If you do not report money that is being refunded or paid to you (either at closing or afterwards), then you most likely are committing loan fraud which typically falls in the felony category. As I mentioned, in my opinion a traditional, full time, full service real estate agent is a better choice.

Question Seven: I think a home buyer should always pay for an inspection or inspections on the property they are buying. If it is not a multiple offer scenario (more than one buyer making an offer on a house at one time) then your offer should have an inspection contingency (that is the Inspection Contingency Form 35 in WA State). If it is a multiple offer scenario, then you would ask the sellers to allow you do a pre-inspection on the property prior to submitting your offer. More on inspections and multiple offers later but in my opinion you should always do an inspection on the property you are buying period.

Question Eight: Pre-qualifying a property means your real estate agent is making sure they have checked in with your loan person and have asked if there are any immediate concerns or limitations to your loan pre-approval that the agent needs to take into consideration prior to touring. If you are doing a special bond loan that has specific allowable geographic parameters, your agent should be asking about this ahead of time. I recently had a client who was doing one of these special bond loans and she had been through two agents prior to working with me. Both agents were obviously clueless as to the geographic requirements for her special loan, as they got her in deals for two houses that did not fall into the required geographic area for her special bond loan. She wasted a lot of time and inspection money all because her agents did not know or check in with the loan officer as to the specifics of her loan. Pre-qualifying also means your agent is checking to make sure any of your personal conditions are not going to interfere, i.e. you have a dog and a condo that is listed for sale and falls into your price range does not allow dogs. This step is not foolproof, but an organized agent takes time to look into these matters ahead of time. This way, everyone's time and money is not wasted looking at and making offers on places that do not meet your loan type requirements or your criteria.

Question Nine: You want to ask about their current client load to make sure your agent is not on her way to overload. Real estate is a high burnout industry. Your agent needs to have boundaries and know when she is reaching her limit. Buyers take time and a good buyer's agent is going to make sure she has the necessary time to devote to you. Some agents might be able to work effectively with eight buyers at one time, others three buyers. There is no magic answer. It is just important that your agent has thought about this and knows their personal burnout limit and knows how to pace themselves accordingly.

Question Ten: If an agent is working with two different buyers (Pam and Nick) and they both want the same thing (i.e. both want a three bedroom house in the Pine Tree neighborhood for under $500,000) then who is this agent really advocating for? *"Oh, I'll call Pam and show her this new listing in Pine Tree because she is easy to reach and we can see it right away."* Or, *"I'll contact Nick and show him the new Pine Tree listing first because we both like coffee and I could use some."* See the inherent conflict of interest? I think it is best to only have one client per price range/criteria.

However, quite a few agents do not work this way. For example, years ago I had a listing and I was representing the seller. It was a hot market, so we solicited multiple offers; i.e. the seller said they wanted to look at any offers on Thursday at noon. We had four offers for this property and one real estate agent was representing two different buyers for this house. I am sure her two competing buyers did not know about each other. I let this agent know that per Washington State law, she could not submit an offer for two different buyers in a multiple offer situation. Technically, she could work with two buyers looking for the same thing but she could not present offers for both of them simultaneously for the same house. So she got another agent in her office to submit her second buyer's offer for the house I had listed. In my opinion, this agent should not have taken on the second buyer whose price/range criteria matched and thus conflicted with one of her current clients. Who was she really advocating for?

As a buyer, I think it is in your best interest that your real estate agent does not have any conflicts with other existing clients. Therefore, one buyer per price range and area is a good rule to follow. Here is a **tip** as to how you can best determine if a real estate agent you are considering working with truly works this way.

Email or call the prospective agent. Tell them you are looking for a buyer's agent to represent you. The agent's first response (without prompting) should be something like this, *"Great thank you for contacting me. In order to make sure I do not have a conflict with any of my current buyers, I need to know what your pre-approval/price cap is? What type of property you are considering, and what your area(s) of interest are?"*

An example of your response would be, *"I am pre-approved for $300,000 and I am interested in two bedroom townhouses in West Beach."*

Right away the prospective agent should tell you if they have a conflict with an existing client or not. If they already have a client who is looking in your price range/criteria then they can ask if you would like to wait or ask if they can refer you to another agent. If they do not have a client conflict, then they should set up a time to meet with you and go over intake materials.

If the prospective agent is not asking for this information right away, without you prompting them, then you can conclude that they probably do not work exclusively with one buyer per price range and area. If you make the mistake and ask the prospective agent, *"Do you only work with one buyer per price range and area?"* then if they are unscrupulous, they will immediately respond, *"Oh, of course I never work with two buyers who are looking for the same thing."* And you will have no real way to verify if this is true or not. If this is important to you, then find an agent who quizzes you about this right off the bat, without you prompting them. You will then know for sure that this is truly how this real estate agent works.

Question Eleven: In my opinion, any buyer's agent worth their salt is going to use some form of a Buyer Agency Agreement (BAA). It shows you they value their time and yours, and it keeps things up front, clear, and in writing. A basic BAA will state your name, the agent's name, and the brokerage name. It will have a start date and an end date, and will note any geographic areas to be excluded. The agreement will spell out that you are agreeing to have this real estate agent represent you in your home buying search and purchase. You are committing to working with that agent and they are committing to working with you. This is a written agreement, not a verbal agreement (which typically in legal world means nothing). Should you discover that you do not like working with this agent or vice-versa then the BAA should be voidable by either party when notice of termination is delivered in writing (via fax, email or mail).

Once that BAA termination is delivered, you are done and can move on to another agent. The BAA protects the agent from having you bait and switch them. For example, you have Mary acting as your agent but you do not have a BAA with her. She spends a lot of time showing you 27 houses. You finally decide that house 26 is the one for you. You then tell Mary, *"Thanks for showing me all of these houses but I am going to have my Aunt Jackie write up my offer for me and be my agent. She just got her real estate license and I feel I need to help her out, but thanks for your time Mary and can I send you a coffee shop gift card for all your hard work?"* Well, bad karma on you the buyer! This happens far more often than you might imagine.

Savvy agents in the 1980s created the Buyer Agency Agreement to help mitigate this kind of defection. If Mary had been using a BAA, then when you suddenly decided to use Aunt Jackie to purchase the house that Mary showed you, Mary's brokerage could then legally collect the commission on that sale if Mary can prove she was the procuring cause of the sale; i.e. she showed you house 26 first while you were actively working with her. It is completely unfair for the buyer to have their relative who is an agent fill out the paperwork and collect the commission for Mary's time and hard work. The BAA helps a buyer because things are above board and stated in writing. With a BAA, the agent then has a legal duty to actively look for properties for you. A verbal statement that you are working together means nothing and that agent has no obligation to be out actively looking for you. So that's a little history as to how BAA's originated and why.

Question Twelve: Form 22-A is specific to the Washington State NWMLS purchase and sale agreement forms. It is the Financing

Addendum. If you do not live in Washington State, your local MLS (multiple listing service) probably has a similar financing contingency form that agents use in your area. The financing addendum should be included with every offer that is contingent upon the buyer procuring financing to purchase the property they are making an offer on.

The information for the blanks on this form should come directly from your loan person. Your real estate agent should never guess at what to fill in on the financing addendum. This is one reason why some deals blow up, because the real estate agent did not instruct the buyer to contact the loan person directly for the deal specific financing information to fill in on their offer. Thus, once the offer is signed around and the loan person gets a copy, they then discover the information filled in on the financing addendum is not going to work for the buyer's loan. Seems like common sense to get this information directly from the loan person when writing up the offer, right? Information on this form usually includes: the percentage you are putting down, the specific type(s) of loan(s) you are taking out to complete this purchase, days you have to make a written loan application, the amount of your loan closing costs and pre-paid items that you want to ask (or need to ask) the seller to pay for. A smart real estate agent is going to require all information entered on the financing addendum, come directly from your loan person. They are going to include your loan person in the offer process, not just dump your signed around paperwork on the loan person's desk, after the fact.

Question Thirteen: Yes, before you go on a house tour, you need to have your loan pre-approval taken care of. If you are buying with cash, a letter verifying funds availability from your banker/finance person needs to be on file. You need to have met with a loan person (information on this process is next) and been pre-approved for a loan. Your pre-approval letter then needs to be forwarded to your real estate agent for their files. Based on what you are pre-approved for, you will determine your search price cap; how much you want to spend. Once this is clear, your agent can set up your search and then you can proceed to tour. It makes no sense to go blindly tour properties with an agent when you have no clue what your pre-approval amount is. That would be akin to shopping for a Bentley when you can only afford a Ford Focus. I call these fantasy tours. Any agent who values their time and yours is not going to take you out on fantasy tours. If they do, then the agent, in my opinion, must be completely bored, desperate, clueless, or all three!

Question Fourteen: Some typical out of pocket expenses that you need to plan for when buying include the money you will be paying your inspector(s), money set aside for your earnest money deposit (explained later) and any other funds you need to bring to close the deal (your down payment) based on your loan person's review and instructions. Yes, you are going to need some actual cash on hand in order to make your home purchase.

<u>Question Fifteen</u>: The information in the real estate agent's buyer intake packet should be educational, informative, and hopefully something they have personally written and customized. The worst case is you do not even get a buyer packet. Or you get one that is four-color, corporate-neutered fluff that looks nice and is provided by the brokerage to the agent and usually it is not very informative. Hopefully the buyer packet information outlines the home buying process for you, includes a sample purchase and sale agreement to review and has other required legal disclosure forms such as the Federal Government's Lead Disclosure booklet. In Washington State you are also required to receive the Law of Agency booklet prior to purchasing. I think it is best you receive all of this information, legally required or not, up front before you start touring and write up an offer. This way you have time to read it and ask questions before you are excited about and distracted by the place you are making an offer on.

<u>Question Sixteen</u>: Are the former client testimonials your agent provides legit? Is there a full name by the glowing rave, not just "J. Smith?" Or worse, a glowing blurb with no name or initials next to it, gee I wonder who wrote that? Just because a nice comment about the agent is supposed to be from a legitimate source does not make it so. This is the same with online reviews. Just because an agent, product, service is highly ranked online does not necessarily mean it is legitimate. There are now companies that agents can hire to do nothing but go online and write rave reviews about the agent. And yes, there are agents who troll the internet and post fake, negative

comments about their competitors. So be discerning. Does the agent you are interviewing have former clients and industry professionals (such as escrow, real estate attorneys, and inspectors) that you can contact directly for a reference if you choose?

Question Seventeen: There are many agents who choose to specialize in a certain area or neighborhood, especially if they mostly work as a listing agent. This would be the specialist agent of Jackal Heights. You know the agent who has her face plastered on every shopping cart in the neighborhood, joins every community committee, and stops at almost nothing so she can plant her for sale yard signs in as many lots in Jackal Heights as possible.

While this agent does have her turf and listings, I think a buyer is better served choosing an agent who works and represents a broader area. Jackal Heights may well be where you want to buy but having someone who also ventures outside of that area and has firsthand knowledge of other areas and properties is in my opinion a better idea. This generalist agent can still represent you just fine if you decide to purchase in Jackal Heights. In fact he can most likely defend you from the Jackal Heights specialist agent if she tries to work both ends of a deal there (representing both the seller and the buyer). This generalist agent can also effectively represent you in another neighborhood. He can pull the proverbial rabbit out of the hat if you are not finding what you like in Jackal Heights. He can suggest other areas and properties he knows of and you might end up finding something better. The agent specializing in Jackal Heights probably is not going to be as knowledgeable of other areas, available properties because she is spending the majority of her time trying to maintain her market share and fiefdom in Jackal Heights.

Back in the old days, (meaning the early 1990s) agents were much more area specific or neighborhood specialists. The reason for this was logistical. Back then, many states did not have electronic key boxes. Keys for listed properties were still picked up and returned to the neighborhood listing office. Listings were not posted online like today. Back then hard copy, black and white listing books were published and delivered to the brokerages once a week. Agents used to literally fight over the office copies of the listing books. That is where an agent found out about new listings, got the latest property status information. It seems hard to believe. When I first started in the business, this was still the common practice; the internet was very new in the real estate industry. Pocket listings and secret deals were much more common. An agent typically picked a neighborhood or small geographic area and specialized in it. Thankfully, the internet changed all of this. Now agents have full access to all member listings posted online at their local MLS, and the public has some access as well. This put a big damper on pocket listings and insider neighborhood deals. Now most listings have key boxes for access so the agent no longer has to go by the local listing brokerage's office when touring or previewing to pick up keys. Thus, a competent buyer's agent can now effectively cover a much wider geographic area.

Question Eighteen: If they were taken to court by a former client, what was the outcome, were they cleared of the charges? Has the MLS disciplined or fined them for breaking rules, any complaints at the department of licensing against them? You can ask these questions directly and someone who is honest and secure will not be offended by such questions. If you ask and they act annoyed, shocked, dismayed, then why is that? Given the reputation that some in this industry have, I think these questions are legitimate and easily answered without attitude if they are on the up and up. Don't feel embarrassed to ask these questions even if the agent is Mr. Luxury Real Estate and has 400 sales a year. You can also search online to see if they have been sued or if there are any news articles concerning something they were involved in that is not above board. It amazes me, the number of people who innocently choose to work with crooks, or former crooks. With a simple Google search and a bit of probing you can have answers to these kinds of questions.

Question Nineteen: In some states a convicted felon or someone who served time in the big house for fraud, embezzlement, assault, walks out of jail and gets their real estate license. Some states now require felony background checks and fingerprint new agents but not all. So be alert and do your homework! There are various online investigative services you can use to look up and investigate anyone from your nanny to your agent and loan person. Some states offer such a service via their state highway patrol website. For a nominal fee, you can look up a person and learn if they have been trouble with the law or not.

45

Question Twenty: There are no strict educational requirements for a real estate licensee outside of the cursory class training hours, exam, and in some states there is a high school diploma or GED requirement. I have worked with agents who barely graduated junior high and others who have PhDs and both were competent. However, I would want to ask about my agent's level of education, what they studied and see from that if it reveals anything about their ability to know the purchase and sale forms, to be able to compose an effective and grammatically correct cover letter, etc.… Look at the writing in their personalized printed collateral that is included in the buyer packet they give to you when you meet. Is it informative, can they convey information effectively? Check out their website, blog, brochure, information sheets. Ask them if they personally wrote that content. Many agents pay to have all written collateral done for them by a third party.

Sample Purchase and Sale Agreement…

Hopefully you will be provided with a sample purchase and sale agreement to review ahead of time. This does not mean you have to become a forms expert, it is written by real estate attorneys after all! But you do need to have some idea what each page that you will be signing and/or initialing means. That is your name you are signing on each page and you are acknowledging your responsibility by signing. I think, the best time to review the purchase and sale agreement information is ahead of time, before you have even started touring properties. Your mind will be clearer and you will be more grounded. By reviewing this sample purchase and sale agreement, you will have a good of idea of what is coming later and hopefully a better understanding of what each page you sign actually means you are agreeing to do or not do. When you find the house you want to make an offer on, you will have reviewed the basic paperwork ahead of time so your level of confidence will be higher and your level of anxiety lower.

I have had clients take the sample purchase and sale agreement and then go meet with a local real estate attorney to review it in detail, prior to even touring properties. You may want to do that or you may want to have your offer written such that you are entitled to an attorney review period after mutual agreement is reached. Some states require real estate attorney reviews, Washington State does not. It is up to you to make this decision. Remember, the sample purchase and sale agreement that you review in advance, when you actually write up an offer, your purchase and sale agreement for that property may have a few forms more or less than your sample packet contained. Each purchase has its own unique requirements. But at least the nuts and bolts of the purchase and sale agreement is in your sample packet and you have had a chance to become familiar with it in advance.

One thing I want to stress, if you have any questions that are of a legal nature, your real estate agent must refer you to a local real estate attorney for those answers. At no time is an agent permitted to answer a question of a legal nature. To do so, would be to practice law. Even if your agent knows 100% what the correct answer to your legal question is, she still should keep her mouth shut and refer you to a real estate attorney. This is also true for any tax and finance questions. You should be referred to appropriate professionals in that field who can best answer your questions. There is nothing worse than the know-it-all real estate agent. No one can know it all in this field. To have an ego that big is boring. It is also dangerous if clients are blindly following that agent's advice in areas they should not be speaking.

Choosing Your Loan Person...

Next up is choosing your loan person. You can choose your real estate agent first or your loan person first or choose them simultaneously. The main thing is that you are thinking for yourself and actively putting together a team to represent you and truly work for your best interest. The same types of issues come up when choosing a loan person as do when choosing a real estate agent. The first thing you should do is take a look at your budget. What is your current monthly expense for your rent? Do you hope to keep your monthly housing payment at the same level as your rent or can you budget to increase (or decrease) that amount?

You have looked at your budget and determined for example that you do not want to spend more than $1,100 a month for housing. You will take that number with you when you visit lenders. I would suggest visiting a few different, local, loan people and see what you think. A great interest rate is important but it is also important that you trust the loan person you choose to work with and that they can actually deliver this great rate/loan they promise you. I would first meet with them in person, not over the phone or by email and fax. This will take more time but I think spending more time up front choosing your team will lead to a better end result for you. Are they organized, responsive, timely? A good loan person is going to ask you

48

what your budget is and how much you would like to spend each month for your housing.

They are probably going to run your credit and see what that is like and then take into account your current income, the current interest rates, the available loan products and see which one best suits your situation. They will issue you a loan pre-approval based on your credit scores and other verified factors. Note, just because they pre-approve you for a $300,000 loan does not mean you will want to spend that much. This is where your budget comes in to play. Based on your good credit, they can pre-approve you for $300,000 but you have determined, via your budget, that $230,000 is the price cap point where you want to max out. This ensures you do not get in over your head with your monthly payment. On paper you are good and they can lend you $300,000, but in reality you know your budget and comfort zone is $230,000. Make sense? You are controlling how much money you are going to spend and making sure you are not exceeding your personal budget. We all know about the train wreck caused by unscrupulous lenders. This is one way not to fall prey to that. A good loan person is going to ask you what your housing budget is, what you prefer to spend every month for your housing payment and work from there.

Avoiding Predatory Lenders…

Here are some **tips** to help you avoid predatory lenders:

1. No one (real estate agent or loan person) can require that you work with someone else in order to work with them. For example, Agent Sue will only be your agent if you do your loan with Zan from XYZ Mortgage or vice-versa.

That is a tie-in and a tie-in is illegal in WA State (check your state law on this if you live elsewhere). They can refer you to Zan and hopefully will provide you with a list of several lender names to consult with but they cannot require you to work with anyone else as a condition of them agreeing to work or not work with you. Also, per RESPA (Real Estate Settlement Procedures Act) it is illegal for a real estate agent and loan officer (or any settlement service provider; i.e. escrow, title, surveyors, appraisers, inspectors) to exchange referrals for anything of value. An example would be your loan person refers you to Bob the agent and in exchange Bob pays your loan person a percentage of your sale's commission or a flat fee to your loan person. That is illegal but it does happen and quite a bit from what I hear. Make sure your people (agent, loan officer) are not doing this as it is not in your best interest as a buyer. You can ask them directly about this when you are interviewing; see if they offer a statement in writing to you up front regarding this issue and RESPA violations.

2. Do not assume that since you know your credit is bad or you have a low income that you will not qualify for a loan from a legitimate lender. Go find out from a qualified loan person what your situation really is. If there are credit problems or other issues, they can advise you as to how to go about fixing things. Stay away from the off-market loan sharks. Avoid schemes where someone is going to front

you the money to purchase and in return you promise to quit claim the title to them once you own. They will then make the mortgage payment while you "rent" from them and eventually become the owner, etc.... These kinds of situations are more than likely shady and it is up to you to investigate. Remember, "*If it sounds too good to be true, it probably is!*"

3. Do not let anyone persuade you to make false statements on a loan application or sign a falsified document.

4. Do not sign any loan document that has blanks that are not filled in. Before you sign, write "*NA*" or "*not applicable*" in any blanks that are not already filled in. If you are signing a page that has writing up top and the bottom half of the page is blank, make an "*X*" mark over the blank area before you sign. This way nothing can magically be filled in on that blank page portion after you have signed.

5. Always insist on a hard copy and/or electronic copy of every single form you sign. You should automatically receive hard copy and/or electronic copies of all forms involved in your transaction (from your real estate agent and loan person) as you go. If you are not getting copies, ask for them. If you have to ask for copies, be on alert as this is either sloppy work, something suspicious or both.

6. Do not let anyone trick you into believing you have committed to a loan when in fact you have not. For

example, signing a disclosure statement does not obligate an applicant to proceed with a loan.

7. Do not sign any document without reading it first. Ask questions about anything that does not make sense before you sign. If it still does not make sense, do not sign until someone can explain it to you to your satisfaction. Just because you do not understand a loan or real estate document does not mean you are stupid. You may have your PhD from Harvard and still find some of this home buying stuff confusing. There are no stupid questions, so ask!

8. If you do not speak fluent English or cannot read English, hire a translator that you trust to go with you for all of your loan and real estate appointments and to review all documents prior to signing. A good agent or loan person is going to insist you do this before starting to work with you and is going to have your translator acknowledge their role and responsibilities in writing.

9. Meet with your loan officer in person. Do not do your loan transaction solely via email/on the phone. It is always better to check out someone you are going to do business with face to face first, before you decide to start working together.

10. Research any nonprofit organization that says it helps buyers. Many are legitimate but some are unfortunately fronts for scammers or unethical people.

11. The loan person is going to speak in "financial-ease." Do not let the finance terms they bat around confuse you or intimidate you. If something does not make sense, ask questions until it does. If the loan person cannot explain a term or something so that you fully understand it, they are probably not the person you want to do business with. Do not get fooled or intimated by big banker terms and lingo.

Loan Fraud...

Unfortunately even after the huge loan debacle and crash of 2008, loan fraud is alive and well today. Please do not get tricked into unwittingly committing loan fraud or be pressured into agreeing to do so. Loan fraud is a serious crime, a felony and it is one of the big reasons for the previous real estate crash. Some common scams that I have seen with my own clients include the following.

A loan officer tells you the only way your deal will go through is for you to create a "short term" rental agreement. This would be if you are already a current home owner and are purchasing a new house and you intend to sell your current house after your new house deal closes. The loan person encourages you to have a friend or family member with a different last name fill out the bogus rental agreement and have you collect a fake rental security deposit. This is usually presented as if there is nothing to it, just business as usual, no big deal. Once your deal closes you of course won't be renting your current property and no one will be the wiser. This is completely illegal! If you agree to participate, i.e. procure a fake lease, then you are directly involved in committing loan fraud. Don't go there! Of course, this kind of scenario is typically presented to the borrower right before they are set to close on their new property, so they are in an extremely stressful situation. If their loan officer cannot deliver their loan as promised, then most likely the buyer loses the house they are purchasing and possibly their earnest money deposit. If they agree to the bogus rent-back scheme their lender has proposed then they are committing a crime. Not a nice situation! In this case, it is best to immediately consult with a real estate attorney and report this to the appropriate state board or committee that oversees the financial institution industry in your state.

Another scam I have seen involved a client's loan person who asked them to have me forge an inspection response form so their loan could go through. In this case, the buyers did their inspection and it was revealed the house needed a new roof; there was no life left in it. The buyers asked the seller to replace the roof prior to closing, via their inspection response form. The sellers refused to replace the roof, so game over. This is when their loan person stepped in and told the buyers to have me submit another inspection response form signed by the buyers, which stated no repairs were requested or needed. He said that way the loan could still go through and they could replace the roof later once they were the owners. Very stupid! Why would the buyers want to replace the roof at their own expense, and this was not something they could afford to do. Fortunately, these buyers fired this loan person and got someone who was ethical to work with. We found another house for them to purchase and all went well; in fact they liked the second house better than the first. No loan person should ever suggest that you and/or your agent forge any forms and submit them to them. That too is loan fraud and I for one will not participate.

Another scam I have seen is when clients of mine had a loan person who had them create false financial documents. They said it was presented to them as no big deal; they were clueless that they were committing loan fraud by doing so. Once I heard of this, we reported it and they went to work with a competent and ethical loan person.

These are just a few examples of what's happening out in the field. Do not fall victim to this and if you encounter a loan person or agent who encourages you to participate in any of this please fire them and then report them. The only way to clean up the industry and keep things like this from happening is for consumers to file complaints and follow up. There is no excuse for this kind of thing and it only serves to further tarnish the real estate industry and perhaps crash the economy again.

Response Time...

It is important when you are interviewing lenders (and agents) that you see how good they are with their response time. Do you receive the information they promised you on time? Once you reach a certain point in your home buying transaction, the entire deal essentially rests upon your loan person delivering what she promised to do. You need a real estate agent that promptly provides you and your loan person with all the necessary signed around paperwork for your deal. You need a loan person who is organized and timely, who can complete the transaction by the agreed upon closing date. This is why your loan person needs to be included and play an active part when you are writing up your offer. In addition to providing you with an updated pre-approval letter that is specific to your offer's terms, the loan person needs to be asked if the closing date you are putting in your offer works for them. If the agreed upon closing date in your deal does not work for your lender then the deal is most likely not going to work. Seems like common sense to me, but the stories I hear every month from loan people about this very issue of not being consulted when client offers are being written is amazing to me.

It is best for you to try and gauge how your loan person ranks on timeliness and responsiveness at the start of your approval process. See how they are when you initially meet with them. If they promise to send you a rate quote or pre-approval, loan program information, is it delivered on time as promised? If not, maybe you want to keep shopping to find someone else who can deliver what they promise on time. A lot of unnecessary drama and stress can be added to your purchase if you have an unorganized loan person who over promises and under delivers. That said, you may find an organized loan person who is prompt in delivering what they promise, but given the conditions in the loan underwriting and processing world, certain factors are sometimes out of your loan person's control. Additional and unexpected information can be requested by the underwriter and sometimes delays occur through no fault of your loan person.

When you meet, a good loan person is also going review with you where the source of some of your funds may be coming from. If you are going to have some of your funds gifted to you by a family member or you are going to be liquidating stocks and having those funds transferred into your checking account, your loan person should review with you up front the type of documentation the underwriter is going to require. For example, if your father is gifting you $5,000 to go towards your loan down payment, then the underwriter is going to require written documentation of these gift funds before they will fund your loan. Getting this specific type of letter written and signed by your father documenting those funds can be time consuming and stressful. A good loan person is going to review this song and dance with you at the start of your home search, so you can get the proper funds documentation for them in advance, not two days before your deal is set to close! I have had quite a few clients put through this mad rush at the very end of their deal to supply funds documentation letters, rent check copies, stock statements, etc.... Much of this last minute drama is unnecessary and could have been avoided if their loan person had been pro-active and organized at the start. Doing this kind of last minute documentation fire drill is not fun for a buyer and it is definitely stressful.

Another point, your agent may know if a certain lender or loan person is good at actually delivering what they promise. I know in my market there are unfortunately a couple of lending institutions that appear to always fail to deliver on the loans they promise clients. Just about every single deal with them ends in disaster because at the last minute they cannot complete the loan they originally promised the client. In fact, how they even manage to do a single home loan is completely beyond me given their blatant incompetence. You might want to ask your agent their opinion regarding the loan people you plan on talking to. Most are fine but there are some that are notorious within the industry for over promising and failing to come through in the end. I can guarantee you this is not something you want to experience.

Institutional Lender vs. Mortgage Broker…

You can choose to get your loan through a bank, credit union, savings and loan (institutional lenders) or through a mortgage broker (independent mortgage shopper). Typically, the institution's loan person does not have to be licensed to do loans and they are usually a salaried employee of the institution. They will be able to offer you loan products that their specific institution currently has available. A private lender or mortgage brokerage usually has loan people who have to be licensed. The mortgage brokers are sometimes paid a base salary plus commission or some work strictly on commission. These brokers are able to shop around the various financial institutions/lenders for loans. Since they are not confined to only offering loan products that their institution has available, they can sometimes find you a lower rate/better loan package. Sometimes they actually broker a loan for a bank, if the bank's rate is the lowest or best deal. So there could be an advantage to finding a broker who can shop around for the best rates for you. Please keep in mind that they need to be able to actually deliver what they promise you. A great loan program/rate is worth nothing if in the end you can't qualify/secure it. I have had satisfied clients who have worked with institutional loan people and others who have worked with mortgage brokers. There is no absolute right or wrong. I would advise shopping around and see who has good rates, who is knowledgeable, and most important who do you trust to deliver what they are promising.

Keep Things Vanilla...

Once you have chosen a loan person to work with and are pre-approved please keep this in mind, never quit your job (try not to get fired) while your deal is pending. The loan underwriter is going to verify your employment on or close to your closing date. If you are no longer employed, then your deal blows up, they won't fund the loan. If you get a promotion, a demotion, a one cent an hour raise, during your home buying process always immediately report that change to your loan person. If you get a great job offer while you are waiting for your deal to close, you should let your loan person know but do not change jobs until after your deal has closed. Underwriters are extremely squeamish about any kind of work related/wage changes that occur between your mutual acceptance date and your closing date. Keep everything as stable and simple (vanilla) as possible. There are true stories of buyers who did not know better and once they were waiting for their closing date, they assumed all was good so they told their boss where to stick it and quit their job. Their loan did not fund, they did not get the house. Don't go there!

Here is another point that your loan person should warn you about. Never open new credit accounts or make large purchases while your home purchase is pending. For example, do not leave your home inspection and since it went really well and you are now sure you are going to go through with the purchase of the house, drive straight to the furniture store and buy new furniture for the house. Large purchases like that before your deal closes are almost guaranteed to completely screw up your loan and more than likely your deal.

Another **tip** which may sound completely counter intuitive is do not close or pay off any existing credit card balances you may have. What? That is right, if you normally have a running balance on your Visa card and it is there when you are pre-approved for your loan, let's say the revolving balance due is $2,000. That is the amount you usually have unpaid on that Visa account each month. You get pre-approved and then have a sudden windfall and decide to pay off that $2,000 revolving balance on your Visa card. Do not do it! Contact your loan person first and let them look at things and advise. Same if you have a department store credit card account that is open but you never use it. Do not close that open and unused credit account while you are in the process of buying/closing your new house. As counter intuitive as this may sound, these things can screw up your loan.

Real Life...

Stories abound from coast to coast regarding the stereotypical, well known, wheeling dealing agent who woos the public and media but within the industry everyone knows they are slimy. Years ago, one of my neighbors found out I was a real estate agent and boy did she unload on me! She was furious because she felt she had been screwed, chewed, and barbequed by her agent. This big name agent had done just about everything I advise not doing. When I asked her why she decided to work with this man her response was she had seen him on TV and on ads throughout the city so he must be good. She found out the hard way that is not necessarily so. She had called up his office, met one of his assistants and was off to the races. They showed her properties before she had even met with a loan officer and gotten pre-approved, much less looked at her budget. He then steered her to "his loan person" who does all of his client's loans. This charming loan shark put her in an interest only loan and a negative amortized loan. He told her she did not need to do an inspection and her loan person agreed.

After moving in, she discovered quite a few issues that she had to fix and pay for that any basic inspection would have uncovered. She never saw any of the required forms, and had no clue what she was agreeing to when she signed her offer paperwork. She was basically charmed and steamrolled straight through to her closing. To this day, when Mr. Bigname Agent has one of his parties she attends. Why? Because in her social circle everyone uses this agent and she does not want to be left out or be the one to say, "*The emperor has no clothes.*" She is also scared to say anything, because of the position this agent holds in her social club. Sad but true and this happens far more than most people might imagine.

THREE

MANIPULATION

The topic of manipulation is very pertinent when it comes to buying a home. The world of sales abounds with manipulators of all stripes. Some are natural born manipulators, others are trained to manipulate. Either way, in my opinion, it is not something that lends credibility to the real estate or lending professions and it is certainly why the generic term "sales" is so reviled in many circles. Please note, not all sales people are manipulators. The manipulator sales stereotype exists for a reason but if you are grounded and take time to organize yourself up front, hopefully you can avoid those who do business by manipulating. Many manipulators are quite proud of their girls' club (I say girls' club not boys' club as most agents and loan officers are female) and over the years the shop talk that I have overheard behind the scenes has curdled my ears! They boast of their manipulative abilities, their ability to "turn" a client, to essentially force their will/agenda on the unsuspecting client.

The buying public is equally to blame for this manipulative dynamic. Many buyers apparently love to have smoke blown at them, be cooed over, praised for their buying smarts, have their vanity and ego stroked and encouraged, while their wallet is being emptied. It takes two to tango! If that is what you enjoy, have at it. But you can be a responsible and informed buyer and find someone to work with who is not always going to stroke your ego just to get the sale. You don't have to choose to work with someone who tells you only what you want to hear; i.e. that a swamp land dump of a house is the next Hearst Castle, your diamond in the rough.

Signs of Manipulation...

Here are some key signs that you might be dealing with a manipulative real estate agent.

1. The agent networks through family, friends, social clubs, religious institutions, and makes you feel obligated to work with them due to your common connection. This is similar to your coworker who is always chasing you down the hallway and popping into your office to try and sell you their latest multi-level marketing product. You know the skin creams, the time shares, the miracle life juice, etc...? They use your common connection and warp your friendship or familial status to essentially force you into using their real estate services. They usually have an aggressively pleasing personality but it is clear your friendship or connection with them is completely tied up in your supporting their business.

2. A friend, co-worker, boss, strongly pressures you to work with their real estate agent. This could be a sign the agent is providing them with a referral fee or a percentage of their commission from your purchase. This is illegal in some states. In the many years I have taught classes, here is the worst story I have heard regarding this item. A woman attended my class after she had signed around her deal and she was set to close in a week. A condition of her loan was

to attend a certified home buyer class. When I got to this item in the class, the woman started crying. She then told the class that when she started to look into buying a house her boss called her in. He told her if she did not use X real estate agent to buy her house, then within 30 days of closing on her new place, he would find a legitimate reason to fire her. Obviously we were all stunned. This is the most blatant manipulative story I have heard, thus far. We asked her why she did not report this to her personnel director or better yet seek legal help. She felt it was best to not rock the boat and go along. Because she had poor boundaries and probably low self esteem, she allowed herself to get brow beat into using an agent she did not care for. I suspect she ended up purchasing something she was not that thrilled with either. Please do not let this happen to you.

3. Your loan person waits until after you are in a deal and getting near to your closing date to inform you that a condition of your loan (or other financial assistance program) is that you attend a certified home buyer class. The loan person should know that attendance to a class like this is required for that type of loan or assistance program when you first meet with them and discuss the loan and/or special assistance program you will be using. Or they may casually mention this class requirement to you at your first meeting but tell you not to worry; you can take care of it

later. Most likely they did not tell you about this class attendance requirement up front or made light of it because they are fearful you will attend one of these certified buyer classes and discover that they and/or your agent might not be the best choice for you to work with. Once you are in a deal and on your way to closing, it is usually way too late to undo your team choices or get out of a deal that might not be the best choice for you. I have taught these certified classes for years and the number of buyers who are already under contract attending these classes continues to soar. The time to take a home buyer class (certified or not) is before you are in a deal, before you have committed to working with a specific agent or loan person. Some class attendees have been told by their loan person or agent, *"Those classes are a joke; a mere formality, don't worry about it."* Most who have attended my class do not agree the class is a joke. They have stated many times in their class evaluations that they wish they had known to take this class before they made an offer and were under contract. In my opinion, if truly educating buyers is the goal of these special loan and nonprofit assistance programs, then they need to walk the talk and require anyone who uses them to take this kind of class before they are under contract.

4. The agent acts like they are your new best friend. They may take you to concerts, treat you to dinner, buy you gifts, anything to land you as a client. While that may feel

flattering, it's manipulative. Find a new best friend somewhere else. This is business first, there is way too much money involved for it not to be. This is not the breezy, light and frothy, *are we having fun yet*, arena. Go find Barbie or Ken elsewhere if you are looking for that. It's not to say you cannot have fun while searching for a house or have a good connection with your agent and perhaps become friends with your agent or loan person after the fact. But again, this is something that requires attention to detail, experience, and for you to wear your grown up hat. Otherwise you might just skim the surface with Barbie or Ken and fun-time your way right into a place you truly regret. Or you may overlook important steps/factors because you are too busy being dazzled and getting a natural high off having fun while buying your house.

5. The agent says they will pay you money for working with them. They may say they will pay (or refund) you money at closing or after closing. These situations can be illegal. Even if they are completely legit, do you really want to work with someone that is either so desperate or incompetent that they have to pay clients to work with them? Does your dentist, accountant, lawyer, etc…, pay you money to work with them? In my opinion, a good agent knows their worth and knows the services they are providing are worth the commission they are earning. The key word there is earning. They work hard and are good at

what they do. Anyone who thinks being a real estate agent is a fun and easy job is gravely mistaken. Rewarding yes, fun at times, but easy, absolutely not. The old saying is true, *"10% of the agents do 90% of the work."* In my opinion, good agents do not need to pay or otherwise coerce people into working with them.

6. An open house agent or new construction site agent tells you that you will not get the house/condo unless you write up the deal with them or you should use them to write up an offer because they can get you a better deal. First, most MLS rules prohibit a member (an agent) from soliciting another agent's client like this. But even if you do not currently have an agent when you visit an open house or new construction site, you would still most likely be better off finding another agent to write up an offer for you on that property. The site agent might be the nicest, most ethical person on the planet but if they are contracted by the developer to sit that site then most likely if they write your offer up it is going to be as a dual agent. That as you know, is not something I think is in your best interest. This would be the case if you attend an open house and the agent holding it open is the same agent as the name out front on the installed yard sign. If another agent from the listing agent's office is holding the house open for the listing agent, then that most likely would not be a case of dual agency, in the sense that open house agent is not hired

by the seller or directly representing the seller. If you tell the agent at an open house or new construction site that you are currently working with an agent and they still persist in soliciting you to work with them, please let your agent know. Hopefully your agent will report them for violating MLS rules. Regardless of rules, that behavior is unethical, you do not poach another agent's client, unless of course you are an unethical, manipulator.

7. A real estate agent keeps showing you properties that are above your price cap point. So you are pre-approved for $300,000 but based on your budget you have instructed your real estate agent to cap your property search at $285,000. You go out on a tour and see places for $199,000, $250,000, $235,000, $285,000, and $225,000 and suddenly your agent suggests you take a *"quick peek"* at this listing right there on the corner that is listed for $299,000. They may say to you, *"It is just a little over your price cap and surely you can afford a bit more."* or *"It is worth looking at and then you can see if you can get it for less."* Wrong! Your agent should respect the price cap of $285,000 that you gave them. If you see everything under your price cap point and hate them all, then your agent might ask if you would like to see what properties up to $300,000 look like. But ask is the key word. They should not be slipping in places in your tour that are above what you have stated you want to pay.

8. Agent does not provide you with client tour reports from the local MLS. These are the client print out sheets which lists the basic information for each property you are going to see. Even with all of today's bells and whistle technology, these sheets of paper are still a great way to take notes on properties as you tour them and refresh your memory later on when you are reviewing your tour. After touring a few houses, they will all start to blur in your mind. *"Which one had the orange counter tops, which one had the avocado shag carpeting?"* I encourage my clients to take notes on these forms, and I take notes on my agent copies of these tour forms as well. This way, later on, I too can recall the house. I usually nick name a place, *"smelly litter box"* or *"avocado shag"* as that is how I best remember things. One side story, I had a client looking for lofts years ago and we were out touring when we came upon *"the panty loft."* We both nicknamed it this on our tour sheets because inside, scattered all over the loft were women's panties of all colors and description. We both concluded a stripper who was a sloppy housekeeper lived there. It was pretty strange but humorous.

You can usually get some version of these client forms yourself online but your agent can provide you with the most up-to-date and usually more complete version from the MLS (which is where most of these independent web sites pull their listing information from). Prior to the internet, manipulative agents used to brag about not giving their clients these tour sheets. Their theory was the more information you the buyer had, the more questions you might ask, and the longer the time to make the sale. Go figure.

9. An agent suggests you do not need to have an inspection for the property you are buying. Run! If you are buying Snoopy's dog house, Trump Tower, a brand new model home, a 90 year old house, always have your offer contingent upon an inspection or do a pre-inspection before making an offer if it is a multiple offer scenario. An inspection is always in your best interest. Most types of loans are going to require you have the property inspected by a qualified (licensed in some states) inspector. Please do not commit loan fraud and forge an inspection report (first hand stories from buyers in my classes, I kid you not). Even if the property you are buying is new construction and an inspection is not required by your lender, it is always in your best interest to have your offer contingent upon an inspection and do one (or more). Let me repeat this, even if you buy a brand new home directly from a developer, and it comes with a builder warranty that last 100 years, still insist that your offer have an inspection contingency. Then pay to have an inspector of your choice check it out. If they try to convince (manipulate) you otherwise, "*You don't need an inspection, it's a waste of money, and time, there is a builder*

warranty, etc…." Fire them! If the developer is secure in what they are selling, then why should they care if you decide you want to pay and have it independently evaluated? I cannot tell you the number of people in my classes that have told me quite proudly that their newly constructed place comes with a builder warranty and their lender/agent told them it was unnecessary for them to do an inspection. Just because something is new and under warranty does not mean there are not serious problems that any competent inspector can find (story on this in a bit). Even if there is a foolproof warranty provided, do you still want the hassle and headache involved if problems are later discovered and have to be repaired; i.e. ripping out drywall to access the faulty pipes? Do an inspection(s) period. An inspection is no absolute guarantee of perfection and later on you might have a faulty pipe and have to rip out the drywall. However, there is a much better chance you will not end up with a problematic property if you pay a qualified inspector to look things over for you. Also, find out how long the new construction developer has been in business. Research their track record. Sometimes developers form an LLC (limited liability corporation) for use in building a specific project. Once that project sells out, they dissolve the LLC. Thus, there is no formal entity left to go back to should things go wrong down the road.

10. Agent does not inform you, prior to touring, that one of the places you are going to see is her own listing. This means her sign is in the front yard and she is representing the seller. If you are interested in that property, it would be a dual agency deal if you agree. And you know, I don't advocate that you agree to participate in a dual agency transaction (one agent representing both the buyer and the seller).

11. Avoid a person who is licensed to be a real estate agent and also approved to be a loan person. These people were around mostly during the real estate boom. By acting as both your agent and your loan person they are trying to make as much money off each client as possible. You can't fault them for that but to do a good job and stay on top of things, I think, you need one person to be your real estate agent and another live human to be your loan person. Two people not one! Real estate and lending are two full time jobs and both are very time consuming and stressful.

12. An agent does not supply you with a sample purchase and sale agreement to read over prior to writing up your offer. As you know, I think it is best you receive this sample packet when you first meet with your agent. A good agent wants you to be informed, to ask questions and feel comfortable with what you are doing. Giving you a sample purchase and sale agreement to review in advance can help with this. A manipulator does not like it when you are

informed or you ask too many questions. They want to keep things light and airy and keep you moving along as fast as possible. If you have time to think or ask questions then you may slow things down for them or worse yet, begin to see through their smoke and mirrors routine.

13. Watch out for the agent that is all personality, smiles and good times. They have charm and charisma and make you feel special, smart, appreciated and everything is always upbeat, sunshine and roses. These characteristics while nice sounding and sometimes fun to be around are usually the typical signs of a manipulator. It is the distinction between charm and manipulative driven sales versus character and informational driven sales. A good agent can have a nice personality/charisma but they also have substance/ethics. They provide you with good, unbiased information so you can make up your own mind about a property. They do not have an agenda or allow their ego to rule your sale. Someone with character does not always tell you (your ego) what you want to hear. That doesn't mean they are rude to you but they politely state the facts or their opinion and then let you decide what is best for you. I love the much touted word "integrity" which the sales world is so fond of using. If someone truly has integrity and works with integrity, they don't typically run around crowing about it every chance they get. Sort of like the old story about those who sing the loudest in church....

CHARLES CHAPLIN

Sometimes I will get buyers who are suffering from what I call "buyer-itis." For example, I had a client who had very rigid criteria, meaning she only wanted to consider available properties within an eight block radius of her current apartment. She had a limited budget as well, so consequently there was only one active listing she could afford that fell within her very small search radius. It was a basement level, moldy, dark, dump of a condo. Its two small windows looked out onto the complex's garbage containers. It appeared to me this dank den had originally been a janitor's workroom way back when this building was originally constructed in 1910. This buyer was completely bonkers about buying this grubby condo. I knew where she currently rented was way nicer. I finally talked her off the ledge and convinced her to not buy. I told her that she would probably turn into a moldy ball of fur living in that place and when I came back in seven years to list her place for sale, it was going to be awfully hard to market a dank, moldy basement pit. She saw reason and decided to hold off on purchasing. From a manipulative salesperson's point of view what I did was idiotic. They are all about short term sales goals and making a sale for the immediate monetary gain. From my point of view, I was thinking client satisfaction and taking the long term view not short term sales goals. In this example, this client greatly appreciated what I did and she sent three excellent referrals to me and then four years later when she was making more money, I sold her a great condo in her neighborhood.

Now for the story I promised you earlier. I mentioned I do not work with family or close friends. A few years ago a friend contacted me and said he wanted to buy a new townhouse. I gave him some agent names and wished him luck in his search. He found an agent who was not on my referral list to work with. I did not know her but it appeared she had been working as a real estate agent since the year I was born, so many years of experience! They found a new construction townhouse and she wrote up his offer. When writing up the offer, he asked her if they should include an inspection contingency. The agent told him that was completely unnecessary as this was new construction, so nothing to worry about and his lender would not require an inspection to complete his loan. Why bother and waste the money? He agreed, so there was no inspection contingency. Next, he asked her if they should note in his offer that the tile work in the kitchen and baths had not been completed and the cabinets had not been installed. She told him not to worry, no need to mention it, the developer would take care of those items. He was correct, a good agent in my opinion, would have included a blank addendum with his offer spelling out in specific detail the work that the developer needed to complete, including model numbers, stains, etc... and specifying all the work be completed at least five days prior to closing. Then the agent and client could check to ensure this work was done when they did their final property walk through (that is five days prior to closing in WA State). He did not ask and his agent did not mention it, so they did not do a final walk through of the property prior to closing. His

75

deal closes 30 some days later and he is now the owner. The agent
gives him the keys and he goes over to move into his new townhouse.

There is no tile work or cabinetry in the kitchen or bathrooms.
He called his agent and she went on about how sorry she was to hear
the developer had not completed the work but it was now out of her
hands. She gave him the developer's number and suggested he call
them directly. He called the developer and they bluntly told him, the
work would not be done, he was now the owner and if he didn't like it
he could sue them. He discovered when he consulted with a real estate
attorney that suing the developer was not really a viable option. So at
his expense, he had the tile work and cabinetry installed.

About six months after moving in, the air conditioning and
heating units began to have problems. These are those dual metal units
that butt up next to the wall; you have probably seen them in motels.
It is very clear what they are, and it is easy to access them. He called a
repair person out and the repair person removed the metal covering
and looked inside the units. It turns out these heating/cooling units
were about 20 years old, so they were at the end of their life
expectancy. Unfortunately, my friend had assumed that since this was
new construction then the heating/cooling units were new as well.
Had he done an inspection, had his offer been contingent upon one,
any competent home inspector would have checked those units and
revealed their age. That would have been a wonderful red flag. What
else might not be new in this new construction project? What might be
hidden or what corners may have been cut? During his inspection
contingency period he could have legally terminated his purchase and

sale agreement and gotten his earnest money deposit back (explained later). He could have had the option to ditch this place and find something else.

The worst part of this story is to this day when friends or family need a real estate agent who does this man refers them to, his crocodile agent! Why? Because this agent pays him $1,500 in cash for each referral he sends to her who closes a deal with her. Talk about karma. It is crazy but this shows you firsthand what I said about making sure you personally vet any agent your best friend or family member refers you to. You never know what is going on behind the scenes. Even if nothing is going on, you still want to make sure you select an agent that you have investigated, trust, and feel comfortable working with.

Hopefully this helps illustrate how manipulators work and what they might do within a real estate purchase scenario. You don't want to become paranoid and cynical. Just make sure you stay balanced and that what you are being told rings true with your real self, not your vanity or ego.

FOUR

WHAT TO SEE

To recap what I suggest you do before you start touring properties, you have:

1. Chosen a real estate agent to represent you and signed a Buyer Agency Agreement with them.

2. Decided who your loan person is going to be and been pre-approved for a loan.

3. Determined, based on your budget, what your search price cap is.

4. Provided your agent with a copy of your loan pre-approval letter.

5. Had your agent contact your loan person and review any loan conditions he needs to know about for properties that will work for your type of financing.

6. Decided what area you want to look in and what your search criteria is, i.e. a two bedroom townhouse.

7. Reviewed the intake packet materials including the sample purchase and sale agreement and asked any questions that you may have.

8. Made sure you have funds in your checking account to cover miscellaneous out-of-pocket expenses (earnest money deposit, inspection).

Types of Properties...

There are basic types of property to consider when purchasing residential real estate. These include:

1. Vacant land
2. Single family residential
3. Townhouses (duplexes)
4. Condominiums and co-operatives
5. Mobile homes
6. Short sales and foreclosures.

When you buy vacant land, a single family style house, a condominium, a co-op, mobile home, a short sale or foreclosure, all of these transactions will require unique transaction forms or addendums specific to their type. You will already have reviewed your sample purchase and sale agreement in advance. In my opinion, your agent should review any property type specific forms with you when you decide what type of property you are interested in purchasing.

Vacant Land...

Vacant land is just what it says; land that is empty and has not been developed. Most people who want to build their own custom house are looking for vacant land to purchase and then build on. With vacant land, your purchase and sale agreement should have a feasibility contingency which gives you an agreed upon period of time after mutual agreement to verify that this land will allow you to build whatever it is you intend. During this feasibility contingency you will be verifying utility connections, septic or sewage requirements, setbacks, architectural reviews, environmental requirements, etc....

Single Family Residential...

Single family residential is usually the term used to describe a house that is detached and sits on its own lot. Visualize a typical suburban ranch style house for this term or a mansion complete with three acres of land around it. Typically single family homes are yours without any association memberships, dues, etc.... That said, some single family homes are in neighborhoods that do require association membership of all home owners and require annual or quarterly fees to pay for the neighborhood association's pool or the security company that patrols the area. Some single family neighborhoods only allow certain lot owners in the development to belong to the local swim club or to have beach rights. Other single family residential associations have restrictions as to what exterior paint colors a home owner can use, types of plants that can be planted in the front yards, even what types of vehicles can be parked overnight at the property.

Townhouses...

Townhouses (or duplexes) are attached to each other and can be considered single family residential. They can be planned unit dwellings or they can also be townhouse style condominiums. It is important that your agent verify exactly what category any townhouse you have interest in falls under so that you use the correct purchase and sale agreement form to write up your offer and so your loan person can verify that your loan type will work for the category the townhouse falls under. Many a time, a buyer purchases a townhome thinking they are purchasing single family residential only to discover it is in fact a condominium form of ownership. It gets a bit tricky because townhouse communities can be planned communities and/or come with association membership and restrictions. Townhomes usually have some kind of association in place whereby the townhome owners agree to have the common areas maintained; i.e. the gutters, roof, driveways, common lawns. So with a townhouse it may be single family residential ownership but also with a mandatory association membership which entails quarterly fees to ensure the common elements are maintained.

Condos & Co-ops...

Condominiums and co-ops are properties that are usually in multi-family style settings. They require the home owner pay monthly (sometimes quarterly or annual) home owner dues to the home owner association or to the complex's management company. With this form of ownership you are going to have your monthly mortgage payment and then another monthly payment to cover your home owner dues. The home owner dues typically cover the costs to maintain the whole complex; upkeep of common areas, trash, water and sewer, in addition to insurance for the complex. The cost of these dues and what they cover varies from one complex to another. Usually with a condo, you are going to have your own utility bills for your unit, the electric, gas and phone or TV connections. The water, sewer and trash bills are usually paid by the management company and costs for these services are typically included in your homeowner dues.

Condo vs. Co-op...

What is the difference between a condominium and a cooperative? With a condo you outright own your unit and with a co-op you own shares in a corporation. The area within your condo walls is literally your property. With a co-op the area in your unit is not your property, you own shares or a percentage of the overall complex. Co-op ownership percentage (shares) is typically figured based on the square footage of your unit and sometimes the floor it is located on. You then have a share in the common ownership of the entire building and have voting rights based on your shares. Typically to purchase a co-op, the board must first approve your membership. Co-ops are more common on the East Coast and they were the precursor to condominiums. Financing for co-ops is not usually an easy thing to procure or at least it is not as easy as getting financing for a condo purchase. Thus, when you own a co-op it is harder to sell because the financing is not as easy for a prospective buyer to get, the co-op board has to approve any potential buyer, and some buyers do not want to purchase shares in a co-op organization. They would rather have outright ownership of their space. Therefore, condos are a more popular (in terms of numbers) than co-ops.

Extra Steps for a Condo...

A condominium purchase has a few extra steps that a single family home purchase does not have. With a condo you will be requesting and receiving a Resale Certificate or if it is a new construction condo project a Public Offering Statement. This should be detailed on the first page of your purchase and sale agreement (in WA State). The seller pays for the Resale Certificate and the accompanying documents, the CC&Rs (covenants, conditions, and regulations). This typically includes all rules, regulations, and bylaws for the condo, board meeting minutes, financial and reserve account information (something your loan person is going to want a copy of), any current litigation against the home owner's association, any special assessments, anticipated repairs, the current owner occupancy ratio, and types of financing the complex is approved for. If there are any pending lawsuits against the association then your loan person most likely will not be able to lend you money to purchase in that complex until the suit is settled.

The seller has to request the Resale Certificate from the management company that manages the condo complex. If the complex is self managed, then a Condominium Resale Certificate Form 27 (in WA State) should be provided to the appointed person who fills out those documents for the self managed complex. The seller will order and pay for the Resale Certificate and CC&Rs (usually $300 to $500) and it can take the management company 10 days, sometimes even longer to prepare it. They will send all the documents to the seller who then has to sign it. The listing agent forwards it to your agent who then delivers it to you. You sign for receipt and in Washington State you have five days to review a Resale Certificate and CC&Rs or if you are purchasing new construction you have seven days to review the Public Offering Statement and CC&Rs. Your lender is going to request a copy of the completed Resale Certificate. Your agent should forward the Resale to your loan person as soon as it is delivered.

During the review period, you need to ask any questions that may come up, verify that the condo rules are okay with you. You would submit any questions directly to the management contact person that is referenced in the documents. They may refer you to a condo board contact person. You need to be getting answers to your questions regarding the condo complex directly from the condo management company and/or the home owner association contact person, not from your agent, the listing agent, or the seller. If for some reason there is a rule or condition that you cannot live with, you can terminate your deal based on the Resale Certificate or Public Offering Statement and CC&Rs review. If your agent keeps you within the review deadline time period and files the paperwork properly then your earnest money deposit should be refundable. I think the Resale Certificate, Public Offering Statement and CC&Rs review process for a condo is a bit backwards but this is how it is currently handled in Washington State.

One thing to note on a new construction condo project, the Public Offering Statement you receive will outline the home owner dues and usually has a basic management budget outlined. It is good to note, that once the project is sold out and the management of the complex is completely turned over to the condo owners, who then typically contract out with a condo management firm to run the place, your home owner dues may increase. It is not usually until a complex is up and fully running for a while, that the true operational and maintenance costs can be known and budgeted for. Here is a **tip**, if you are buying a condominium make sure you are going to actually use any of the included "*resort style*" amenities. That would be listing agent prose for anything from an algae ridden community hot tub to a gleaming Olympic size swimming pool and gym. If the condo complex comes with amenities, then ask yourself are you really going to use them? Not fantasy land, where you think that you will move in and get in shape, lose 30 pounds by using the condo gym every day. The novelty usually wears off. If you are truly going to use the included amenities then great, if not then maybe you want to look at condos that do not come with all the deluxe community features. You are going to pay for the amenities, via your home owner dues, whether you use them or not. The spas and workout rooms have to be maintained (hopefully) and more important the home owner association has to have a liability policy to cover them. Those policies only increase in cost. Those associated costs are then added onto everyone's home owner dues. I had clients who purchased a condo many years ago and they were extremely excited because the complex had a steam room and they planned to use it every week. When I came back eight years later to list their condo for sale, this couple had actually forgotten their complex had a steam room! They found it hilarious when I was filling out their listing paperwork that they had forgotten about the steam room. Turns out they had used it for the first month or so and then over the years they forgot about it.

Mobile Homes…

Mobile homes (also called manufactured homes) are usually considered to be personal property by a lender. That is if they are not permanently attached to land. Lenders will not usually offer financing for a mobile (or manufactured) home until it is permanently attached to a piece of land. Even then, they will sometimes only lend money for the land. Thus, if you are thinking of purchasing a mobile or manufactured home you will need to first find out if you are actually purchasing the land underneath it or is the manufactured home considered personal property? Even if you are actually acquiring land ownership within the mobile home park, the lender will still require proof that the home (mobile or manufactured) is permanently attached to the land, secured/tied down. This is one reason why mobile home park prices and manufactured home prices are usually less than say the single family, ranch style homes a couple of blocks away. Mobile or manufactured homes can actually be quite nice inside and have come a long way from the stereotype that may come to mind. However, they do not typically appreciate in value as quickly as other types of homes/condos because it is usually harder for a buyer to get financing to purchase them.

Short Sales & Foreclosures...

This is unfortunately a topic we have all heard about far too much in the past few years. A short sale is when the owner of a property is short the money needed to pay off their existing mortgage (loan) when they sell their house. For example, a seller purchased his house two years ago for $400,000 and now is being relocated and needs to sell. The current state of the market dictates that his list price should be $300,000. Thus, he is short $100,000, plus the sale fees and taxes involved in listing and selling the property. He does not have money on hand to make up the difference at closing. Thus when he lists his home, his agent will indicate it is a short sale. This means if the seller gets a full price offer of $300,000, he must then negotiate with the lender (the holder of his mortgage) to forgive or write off all or a portion of the outstanding $100,000 he still owes. There are now short sale negotiators involved in these transactions, in addition to the agents and attorneys.

From a buyer's perspective, short sales take a great deal of time to close and usually cause the buyer much anxiety. Most lenders with whom the seller has to negotiate with to facilitate the short sale, will require a buyer to submit their offer and promise not to make offers on other viable properties while they wait for the seller's lender to do their bureaucratic review and respond to the offer. This usually takes months, sometimes six to eight months. You the buyer are left hanging while the seller's lender reviews and works their muggle magic. There is a good chance your loan pre-approval will expire during this waiting period and your loan rates and terms most likely will change during the waiting period. So four months later when the seller's lender finally comes back and counters your original offer at a higher price, you the buyer might not be able to move forward because the interest rates are now higher or something else has changed to cause your original loan pre-approval package to no longer be viable. It is a long and frustrating process for all involved. Why do it unless you absolutely have to? In most markets, there are still plenty of non short sale properties to choose from, so why put yourself through this? Also, short sales do not usually end up being the awesome bargain you might originally think them to be. The seller's lender often comes back and says your offer price must be increased or they change other terms in your offer.

Foreclosures are sales where the lender has actually repossessed a property and is now reselling it. A seller defaults on their mortgage, can no longer pay and is booted out of the property. Foreclosures are not something a lender (bank) usually wants to handle and they typically do a bad job doing so. Foreclosure (or bank owned) properties are notorious for neglect and damage. In many cases, all of the utilities have been turned off and the property has sat empty without running water, heat, air conditioning for a long period of time. That is not good at all in terms of maintaining a property. Bank owned properties do not have to, nor will they, provide a seller disclosure statement. As a result of all of this, most foreclosure properties are sold to hard core real estate investors who are keen on flipping them or renting them out as quickly as possible. Foreclosures may be priced low, in terms of the current state of the market average price, but that low list price is usually bid up by serious real estate investors who specialize in snapping up these types of properties. The average buyer cannot usually compete against the serious and moneyed real estate investor.

These are just some of the reasons I do not advise purchasing a short sale or foreclosed property. For what it is worth, in my own personal buying and investing in real estate I have always avoided these types of properties. I really do not want the drama and headache that is almost always involved in these types of transactions. This is not to say that some average buyers do not sometimes succeed in purchasing them but that road is usually extremely bumpy and stressful and they often do not end up with the great bargain they originally anticipated.

There are quite a few good ideas floating around to make short sales and foreclosures easier and more consumer friendly but for now I personally avoid them.

What to Tour...

Now you are finally ready to go out and tour properties. Your agent will set up a search for you in the MLS and forward active and applicable listings to you. When I initially set up a client's search, I usually email the client all of the available listings that match their criteria, even if I know some of them my client will have zero interest in. They get the good, the bad, the ugly, and the in between. The client then has a complete overview as to what the current market is for their price cap and area. You might receive an email from your agent with a link that has 20 listings. You scroll through and can quickly delete the obvious duds and you are now down to 12 listings. You map the 12 listings and narrow it down to nine. These nine are now your list of interest. You should then do a drive-by of these nine listings and see what your thoughts are from the car, what the curb appeal literally is. After the drive-by, you might have narrowed things down to five listings. This is the short list you should provide your real estate agent.

Your agent will then hopefully recheck those five listings and see if they are all indeed still active/for sale and if anything has changed regarding price, terms, etc.... Then your agent should study the agent detail reports for these listings (available per their MLS membership) and see if there are any new agent remarks or potential conditions that your loan person may not be happy with. Your agent may contact your loan person again to verify per the online report that a certain property is okay for lending. Your agent might also contact the condominium's management company to clarify that your 40 pound dog is permitted in that complex. So from those five listings there are now four left which are viable. This is your tour list.

Your agent will arrange a date and time for you all to tour these four properties. Some properties require advance appointments, others do not. Your agent should be taking care of this and leaving messages/making advance appointments where required. If it becomes clear that your agent is not doing this (i.e. you keep interrupting sellers at home who are surprised and annoyed to see you as they requested an advance appointment for all showings) then you should consider getting rid of your agent. Any agent who is not polite or smart enough to set up a tour and make advance appointments where they are required, really is not someone you want to work with. What other rules or details are they going to blatantly ignore or overlook on your end of things? And if your agent annoys the seller and you end up making an offer on that property, the seller's first association with you/your offer is, "*Oh it's an offer from the buyer with that rude agent who barged in on us Sunday morning without first making an appointment.*" Despite what reality TV may show, manners and consideration for others actually does work in your favor, even in business.

Of the four properties you tour, two are of the most interest. Depending on how hot or fast moving the market is you may or may not have time to ponder the top two properties. Ideally you have some time to mull it over. I suggest driving back over to the houses and walking the neighborhoods, talk to any neighbors you run into. See what each area feels like. Check them out at different times of the day and night.

If nothing on this tour floats your boat, then your agent should continue searching for you and will forward you new listings as they appear.

When you are touring, a good agent is going to provide you with feedback. They are not going to unlock a property and tell you to look around while they plop down on the front steps and have a smoke. Hopefully they are not following you in the house while gabbing away on their phone or neurotically texting. They should be quietly observing you, not following close behind and literally breathing down your neck or even worse constantly chattering and commenting, *"And here's the stove, I just love a gas stove and they cook so much better I think and look over there is a built-in china cabinet. My grandma Pearl had one of those and when we were children we were not allowed to touch it. Oh and looky here, a double door, stainless steel, refrigerator. My cousin Lucy has one of these and you know she just...."* Blah, blah, blah, please shut up and let me think! Hopefully your agent is pointing out to you helpful things like, *"You know Mr. Buyer, every place we have toured today that has a balcony, you have walked right over to it and commented on how much you like it. Your search criteria does not include a balcony; do you only want to see properties from now on that have balconies?"* Something like that, feedback that is constructive and helpful.

Here is a point to keep in mind. As you are touring your agent will most likely be accessing the property via an electronic (in some

91

markets) key box. If it is an electronic box, then your agent's information is sent to the listing agent so they know who accessed the property and when. Your agent is also required by law to leave their business card in the house. The listing agent and seller should know your agent has been through the property. Accordingly, a good listing agent is going to email your agent and ask for feedback. They will ask if your agent was showing the property to a client or previewing. Then they will ask what the agent and you the client thought of the property. Most will ask for an opinion on the list price. A good buyer's agent will never provide an answer for this price question. Why is that? This story will explain.

I was a listing agent a few years back for a house and I sent out my feedback email on the property to an agent that had just shown it, letting her know my sellers had requested and appreciated any feedback on the property. She responded back with detailed answers. She said her buyer was very interested in the house and regarding the list price question, stated the buyer and she both thought it was priced right. I relayed this feedback to my sellers. A day later the buyer's agent submitted an offer. They offered less than the list price, although via the latest active/sold comps the list price was of fair market value. My seller countered back at full price. The seller cited the agent/buyer's feedback from the previous day, i.e. that the list price was accurate. What more could the buyer or their agent say? The comps showed the list price was good and they themselves said it was an accurate price. Game over! My sellers got full list price. Hopefully this shows you why your agent or you should never provide an answer when a listing agent or seller asks what you think about the list price.

Touring Tips...

Over the years and many clients and classes later, here are some common touring **tips** I can give you.

1. I am often asked, *"How many properties should I look at before I make an offer or what is the average number of properties that most people look at before making an offer?"* I always say that is completely subjective and case specific to the client. Unfortunately I cannot give you a neat and tidy answer. I have had clients who have walked into the first place we tour and know right away they want it and we immediately go write it up. Others look for months and seem to make no progress and then suddenly they tour a place and are ready to write up. Sometimes people are indecisive or scared. Similar to the first time you jumped off the pool's high dive. Scary to make yourself do it but once you did, you wonder what the big hang up was all about. Only you will know when you are ready to write up. That said, I can tell when certain clients have mental blocks or a psychological issue going on that is interfering with their decision making process. In those cases, I have referred clients to psychologists who have helped them. And helping them does not necessarily mean they always buy. Which leads to...

2. Baggage. No matter how Zen master you may think you have become, we all have personal baggage of some kind. For whatever reason without fail, buying a home brings this personal baggage to the surface. A good agent is aware of this and knows how to guide you through it. I always say your long lost inner two year old resurfaces when you are buying a house, so be prepared. If you are a couple buying together, do not freak out if you start fighting like cats and dogs. This is almost a built-in part of the home buying process. Your agent can help mediate. Some of this is due to different information processing styles that hopefully your agent is aware of and knows how to translate.

3. As I said at the start of this book, I have sold everything from mobile homes to mansions. No matter how large or small someone's budget is I can guarantee you that no property is going to 100% perfectly match your wish list of must-haves. It is not to say you can't find your dream home, but there is always something that is not quite completely "right." Welcome to planet earth, perfection does not exist. This is not to say you should lower all expectations and accept a moldy dump but you need to be realistic and take into consideration what your budget will get you. There is no need to be angry because *"those rich people"* get everything they want in their houses. Not true, they get quite a bit but no one gets every single item on their wish list.

4. If you are more open and not so rigid with your must-have criteria and are able to think outside of your expectation box, you may end up with something far better than you could imagine.

5. Stay open and optimistic but remain grounded. Law of attraction is great but if you have a beer budget and think you are going to somehow manifest and score a terrific mansion, well you are dreaming. You might very well manifest/find a terrific house within your price range but it is pure fantasy to think you are somehow going to get a seller to sell you their million dollar home for $100,000.

6. If you miss out on a house, someone beats you to the punch with an offer before you can decide to make one then keep this in mind, "*If not this, something better.*" That is a good mantra to repeat throughout the whole home buying process. Try to flow with things and see what happens. That does not mean be a doormat but try and detach a bit.

7. When you are touring a property, please do not rifle through the owner's underwear drawer, try on the sellers' clothes, plop down on their bed and take a quick nap, help yourself to a soda from their refrigerator, investigate the contents of their medicine cabinet, ignore posted signs from the listing agent (i.e. do not unlock this door), smoke in their living room, move their furniture around, etc.... You are in someone else's house, you should treat it with

respect and how you would like a stranger to treat your house and things.

8. Do not try to operate and/or test the appliances, the programmable thermostat or other gadgets in the house when you are touring. If you make an offer and it is accepted then your inspector can test those items (those that come with the property) for you when he or she (yes there are female home inspectors) does your property inspection. When touring the adage, *"You break it you bought it"* applies. So please leave the items listed above alone.

9. If you have children, try and get someone to keep them for you while you are touring. Touring is more work than you might imagine and children can be distracting. After about two houses they have usually had enough. You can bring the children along to see the house when you do your inspection if you wish.

10. Wear shoes that easily slip on and off, no laces! Most properties now request you remove your shoes. Even those that don't request it, if it is rainy and muddy outside it will be best to remove your shoes so you don't mess up the seller's floors.

11. Do not bring food, drinks, lit cigarettes, pipes, bongs, etc…, with you in a property you are touring. 'Nuff said.

12. If there is a pet in the property and they are confined to one room or in a cage, leave them there! Do not go open

the bunny's cage and let him out so you can watch him hop around.

13. If the listing agent or seller has left a bowl of candy out near the house flyers, feel free to help yourself. But do not feel free to empty the entire bowl's contents into your purse or backpack. Remember the thing about manners?

14. Unless there is a sign telling you not to, it is usually okay to use the bathroom when you are touring a house. That said, please do not feel free to fill up the bath, jump in and test it out.

Real Life...

When I first started out in real estate, I was the buyer's agent for a well known, luxury residential real estate agent. This agent attracted big name clients from around the world and brokered some of the biggest deals in the area. I was the one who actually took the big name buyers out in the field and showed them the mansions, helped them narrow down their choices and helped them write up their offer. Many of the clients were well known entities and discretion was paramount. So, a wealthy, big name person contacted the luxury agent I worked for and arranged to have his wife fly up and for me to show her around. She came with her own limo and driver. That sure made my life easier, having "Hans" do all the driving! She was a nice woman, well dressed, glamorous looking. We had seen a couple of pricey pads when we arrived at our third showing. The listing agent was required to be present at all showings for this estate, so she was there to greet us and left us alone while we toured the property.

97

When we got to the master suite, my buyer went completely nuts over the sunken soaking tub located in one part of the enormous master bath. She asked me if she could try it out. Try it out? I said sure, and turned on the faucet, ran some water to show her how it worked. She looked at me like I was crazy and said no, she really wanted to get in and try it out. She was sore from flying and traveling and wanted to see firsthand how good this soaking tub was. I told I didn't think that would be a good idea. I was quite certain the listing agent would not approve as this is not something a typical home buyer does when touring a property.

The client then asked me to go check with the listing agent downstairs about a question she had regarding the pool house. She was curious as to how high the height restriction might be in terms of adding a second story to it, a point that had been mentioned in the listing report. My client said she would wait in the master suite and take it all in while I went and got the answer to the pool house question. Downstairs I went and it took me a while to find the listing agent. I asked her about the pool house height restriction and the listing agent said she would come back up with me to show my client, via the master bedroom window, where exactly the height restriction for the pool house maxed out.

We wound our way back upstairs and into the master bedroom suite but my client was not there. I couldn't figure it out and then I noticed the doors to the bathroom were shut. We went up to the doors and could hear the water running in the huge soaking tub. I knocked on the door, the listing agent tried the knobs but the doors

98

were locked. When we called out, the buyer shouted out, *"Oh, just wait a bit I'm trying out the soaking tub. I should be done in 30 minutes and then you can show me the height restriction for the pool house. Does the seller have any extra bath salts?"*

This was a first for me and the listing agent. Neither of us were very impressed. So please, even if you are dripping with money and think you are the most powerful beast on the globe, have some common courtesy and restraint and do not test out firsthand the seller's bath tub!

FIVE

MAKING THE OFFER

After touring the listings that were on your short list, you may find that one property stands out and you feel this is the place you want to make an offer on. This can happen on your first tour out or in extreme cases it can happen a year and half later after countless tours and agonizing! When you know you want to make an offer on a property, there are basic steps you are going to want to do before you actually put the pen to paper or in today's world the curser to the auto click blanks.

Neighborhood Review...

Once you have it narrowed down to the property you are most interested in, you need to investigate the area and do your neighborhood review. In Washington State, the Inspection Contingency Form 35 has a box on page two that your agent can check that entitles you to a three day neighborhood review period after mutual acceptance (when your deal is mutually signed and agreed to by both you and the seller). The only time I can think when you would not want this neighborhood review box checked is in a multiple offer scenario. Otherwise, checking this box gives you one more legal way to terminate your deal should you change your mind. All of that aside, the time to actually do your neighborhood review is ahead of time, before you make your offer. You should investigate the neighborhood on your own. If you try and speak with the neighbors and your agent is with you, they are most likely not going to tell you very much. Most people will not speak candidly when your agent is with you. Walk around the block, talk to everyone you come across. Tell them you are considering making an offer on the house down the street. Ask them if they enjoy living in the area. You'd be amazed what people will tell you, some of it you probably don't want to know! You should knock on the immediate neighbor's front door and see if you can speak with them. If they slam the door in your face, do you want to live next to grumpy for the next 10 years? If you are shy about doing this, then get your motor mouth, ex-cheerleader friend to come with you and let her quiz everyone for you.

Next, walk in the neighborhood in the early morning and evening. Does it feel safe to you? Talk to clerks at the nearby mini marts or coffee shops, see what they have to say about the area. Test your commute to work, does the bus you are planning to take really show up on time? Is the 20 minute car ride to work that you plan on making really that easy on a weekday morning? You can look up the crime statistics for the area online but I still advise finding the local police precinct station and speaking in person with the Community Patrol Officer. This officer can usually show you the crime statistics for the area but they also might be able to tell you more than what the paper reports state. If you have children and they are going to attend public school, make an appointment to meet with the principal of the school that area is zoned for. Do you like what is going on in that school, would you want your children going there? How close are the nearest libraries, banks, grocery stores or any other places you frequently go?

Comparison Reports...

Once you have done the above neighborhood review work and you are now confident you want to put in an offer, your agent can pull up property comparisons on the MLS and print out active and sold comparison reports. These are also referred to as comps, a CMA or a comparative market analysis. Usually they are single page reports that show you statistical averages for like properties in the area you are making an offer. The agent can pull up the house you are most interested in and run a quarter mile (sometimes larger if nothing pulls) radius search around the house you are interested in making an offer on. The active comp report will pull up any similar houses in a quarter mile radius that are currently listed (active). For example, the house you are interested in is two bedrooms, two baths and priced at $325,000. Your agent can do a radius search around that house for other two bedroom, two bath houses. It will pull up some properties that were probably on the initial list your agent sent you to review. The active comp report could also contain some listings you have not seen because they are priced above your price cap (example, a two bedroom, two bath house listed at $345,000 one block away). This active comp report will show you what else is currently for sale in the immediate area that is similar to the house you like. It will give you an average list price so you can see how that average area list price compares with the list price of the house you are interested in. Is the house you like overpriced? Based on the active comps, is it listing for more than the average area list price because it has upgrades, it looks like a show pony, or it just feels better than the other houses?

Next, your agent can run another sheet for sold comps. The same process as above is used but it is run for properties that have sold in say the last three or six months, sometimes farther back depending on how slow the market has been. Obviously, the most recent sales will have the most bearing. This sold comp sheet will show you similar sold properties, what they originally listed for and what their posted sale price was. How does the average sale price compare with the list price of the house you are interested in? Is the house you are interested in listed for more money than the average sold comp price because the market has heated up since that last sale three months ago? Is the house you like listed for more because it has upgrades, looks picture perfect? Or is this property overpriced for no logical reason? It could be the sellers insisted on listing the house for more than the listing agent knew (and hopefully showed) it was worth, which is a complete waste of time and money on the seller's part. If you are a Curious George, you can read more about this in my seller's book Home Selling for Smarties. Anyway, these active and sold comp sheets give you a statistical overview of the place you are interested in and show how it compares with other like properties in the area.

When your lender orders your appraisal, most appraisers are going to use this same or similar active/sold comp report technique as part of their process when determining if the price you are paying for the property is realistic, at fair market value. Personally, I have never yet had a client's deal not pass appraisal. I think that is in part because my buyers review active and sold comp data and thus their offers are typically in the realm of reality, so there is no need for the appraiser to claim that the agreed upon sale price is not realistic. I also take time to familiarize myself with any specific conditions my buyer's type of loan may require in advance, so hopefully they can be corrected before the appraisal is done.

For example, with certain bond loans or sometimes with an FHA loan I know there are conditions at a particular property which will have to be addressed and fixed by the seller before the appraiser is going to green light the transaction. Therefore, when writing up the buyer's offer, we can include some of those known conditions and have them addressed hopefully prior to the client's inspection or shortly thereafter. That way, when the appraiser does show up, the conditions that would have triggered the appraisal not clearing have been corrected and all is good. Being pro-active with these kinds of known conditions can greatly reduce the level of anxiety and potential delays in a transaction. However, not all conditions that cause an appraiser to red light a sale can be known or addressed ahead of time.

Now you have your active/sold comp reports and can see firsthand what the statistics show you about the house. Next, you will want to check in and see what your intuitive side has to say. How did the house feel, what is the charm factor compared with other properties you saw? What is the potential to make this house what you ultimately want to live in? Does it feel like a place where you can be happy or at least content? Does this property match what you can foresee yourself needing in the next five to seven years?

Low-Ball Offers...

A final word on deciding what your offer price is going to be. I would avoid the temptation to make a low-ball offer. By that I mean, you can see from the active/sold comp statistics and from your tour that the property you like, its market value most likely is $300,000. In my opinion, it would be really unwise to then make an offer of say $265,000. Why? You might expect the seller to automatically see your low-ball offer as a jumping off point, an invitation to haggle. That might be more valid in certain market regions but usually a low-ball offer will backfire on you.

The seller's ego is tied up in their property and your low-ball offer is often taken as a personal insult. The seller may become so annoyed that they throw away your low-ball offer and do not respond at all. If their listing agent can talk the seller down off the ledge, the seller most likely will counter back to your low-ball offer at full price. So you have insulted the seller and if they do counter your low-ball offer, they really are not going to be enthusiastic about you or this deal going forward. You also could have this backfire on you when you do your inspection and discover there are some reasonable items you want to ask the seller to address prior to closing. If the seller already does not like you because of your low-ball offer strategy, you stand a good chance that they will refuse to repair any items you request be fixed, via your inspection.

It is up to you how to proceed with your offer but low-ball offers, in my experience, do not usually reap the monetary break you desire. Think about it, if the statistics and the market show the list price is fair and what it should be, it is extremely doubtful a seller is going to go for a low-ball offer and take way less than what the current market value is. Would you, if you were in their shoes? If you are making a low-ball offer because you enjoy the thrill, the sense of power you get, then you might want to put your ego in check or seek professional help. Show off/bully egos might work on TV but no one likes to work with that when they are negotiating the sale of their home.

A side note, your agent is the messenger for your offer. You run the show and decide what the offer price should be. You can ask for your agent's opinion but they should not be telling you what to do no questions asked. It is illegal for your agent to refuse to present your offer because she feels it is too low or there is something else she does not agree with you about in your offer. It has zero to do with how she feels or her ego. Your agent has to fill in the blanks per your instruction (unless you are instructing her to break the law) and present your offer. That said if you continue to write up frivolous and insane offers your agent is probably going to terminate your BAA and move on.

Offer Price...

I always advise my clients to put on the seller's hat when they are deciding what their offer price is going to be. How is a seller going to view this offer and why? Your agent will most likely ask the listing agent why the sellers are selling/moving. Occasionally you might get a snippet of insider information from that query. However, smart listing agents are going to provide a polite non-answer, "*They've decided to move on; they want to be closer to their kids,"* etc.... It is very rare your agent will get a response, *"The owners hate the house and the lousy neighbors, they are in the process of separating and it is very bitter,"* etc.... No listing agent should reveal any personal information about the sellers unless instructed to do so by the sellers.

Next, look at your active and sold comp sheets. What do the statistics show you about the list price? When was the most recent sale on the comp sheet, a month ago, six months ago, longer? The more recent the latest comp sale, the more valid it usually is. What is the current state of the market since that last sale? Has it shifted and it is now more of a seller's market, a buyer's market? Are there any known items that you are hoping to get the seller to fix via your inspection report/response? One question that some want answered is, *"What did the seller pay for the property?"* It may seem counter intuitive but that question is not very helpful in determining what your offer price should be. The seller could have purchased the property back in 1976 or purchased two years ago. Regardless, the current state of the market is what you are in right now and it is going to dictate what the sale price is for the house you are interested in. The seller may have purchased the house 40 years ago and is making a huge profit, good for them. If they purchased recently and are barely breaking even at their list price point, *them's the breaks.*

After reviewing the statistical data found on the active and sold comp sheets, you should take into consideration the non-linear factors. How does the space feel compared with other properties you toured? What is the charm factor, the upgrades, is this house the neighborhood show pony? How is the layout, the Feng Shui, the daylight exposure? I could easily write another book on the energy of various properties, creepy things that have cropped up over the years when touring. The main thing is that you are sure the energy or feel of the property is a good match for you. How's that for woo-woo?

From your perspective, the buyer, you need to have a sense of the current state of the market and more specifically the state of the market where you are buying not in the whole metro or state region. What they tell you about your local real estate market on TV is not necessarily applicable. Typically the media reports on real estate trends that are peaking or fading. They tend to be a bit behind the reality of the current state of the market. Also, they usually are reporting in a broad brush sense. Meaning, they might be reporting on hot home sales within the city but where you are interested in buying, 30 minutes outside of the city in a bedroom community, the market conditions might not be as hot as in the city or vice-versa. Even more specific, what is the state of the market for this neighborhood? Some neighborhoods remain hot in down turns; others are slower, or faster than surrounding neighborhoods. Look at the information I have outlined (statistical comp reports and the intuitive feel) and come up with what you think is a realistic offer price for the property. Whether or not the seller is making or losing money on the sale of the property really does not apply. The current state of the market is the ultimate deciding factor. I have had clients say to me when writing up, *"Well we are good people, so we think the seller will prefer our offer and it seems like they would be willing to take less money knowing we'll be living in their home."* That would most likely be delusional thinking at work! The sellers might think you are the sweetest things since apple pie but when it comes down to the money, don't kid yourself.

When you write up your offer you are likely going to have some butterflies in your stomach or sweaty palms. However, if you are throwing up, passing out, or crying hysterically (all things I have encountered with buyers) then you need to stop and see what is going on. Are you getting sick to your stomach and barfing all over the conference room table because of food poisoning or nerves? Are you fainting at the table due to low blood sugar or are you so scared you are just checking out? Are the hysterical tears of joy or are they coming from utter terror? Any of this occurring because of a fear reaction, means this is not your time to write up an offer. In fact, you probably need a long holiday to clear your mind, it's too much. Also when you write up your offer, please do not ask your agent to cross out certain verbiage in the standardized purchase and sale agreement forms. Your agent is not allowed to do that. They should not be altering any of those forms' boiler plate language as only a local real estate attorney can do that. Your agent can craft very simple custom language in your offer via a blank addendum or on counter offer forms but anything that is remotely complex or legal, requires a local real estate attorney to provide the correct verbiage.

Another item to mention when writing up your offer, please do not show up drunk or stoned. You need to have your full wits about you. Party all you want, just do not mix it with your offer/purchase time. The very first deal I ever wrote up, the man buying was old enough to be my grandfather. We sat down at the table to start the paperwork and he pulled a bottle of whiskey out of his blazer and proceeded to gulp it down. I can still see the younger version of myself standing there, trying to politely ask him to put the whiskey away, and to please come back later when he was sober to write up his offer. That is one of the advantages of getting older, because today I would not hesitate to boot him out and firmly tell him he needed to sober up first before writing up his offer. Writing up an offer when you are buzzed or inebriated is not in your best interest, do not do it. And please do not sit down with your agent and hit the bottle or bong together when you are writing up. An agent is not supposed to be partying while they are working with a client.

Multiple Offers...

If the market is hot when you are buying and the housing inventory is low and lots of people are buying, then you are in a seller's market and more than likely there are going to be multiple offers. Multiple offers means that more than one person is making an offer on a property. How this can work is the seller, via their listing agent, will state (usually in the online listing report) something like, "*Seller to review all offers, if any, on Thursday, March 15 at 5 p.m.*" This means they are trying to set up and/or anticipating several buyers making an offer on the property. So you know things are going to be more competitive. You need to review with your agent, the best strategy for this multiple offer situation. Here is what I typically do with my buyers in this situation. There are other things that can be done and each multiple offer situation is unique. It requires your agent and you use your best judgment and intuition.

1. Do a pre-inspection on the property. You have to get the seller's permission first. You pay for an inspector to look at and evaluate the property before you make an offer. This way you know the condition of the house before you offer and you can make your offer without an inspection contingency. Why do this? Because competing offers most likely will not have inspection contingencies. That contingency draws things out five or seven more days. Those are days the seller does not like tying their property up. If the seller can avoid doing so, they would prefer that.

2. Increase your earnest money deposit (explained in minute). This is more of a psychological ploy but it can look good on paper.

3. Increase your down payment.

4. Tighten up all of your contingency timelines, i.e. your financing timeline if possible.

5. Do not ask the seller to pay for any of your allowable pre-paid or closing cost items via your financing addendum.

6. If the comps show the list price is close to where it should be, offer full list price. Obviously do not do that if the list price is overinflated, via the comps.

7. Possibly do an Escalation Addendum 35E (in WA State). This will detail how much over a competing offer's best price you are willing to go in order to get the property.

Typically escalations are in $1,000 or more increments and you of course indicate your escalation price cap. Example, your offer is for the list price of $320,000 and your escalation clause is for $1,000 over any competing offers up to $350,000. You beat out the competing offer and the purchase price ends up being $346,000. Your agent should get a complete copy of the closest competing offer, per the terms of the escalation addendum, to verify in fact that $346,000 is correct and the closest offer maxed out at $345,000. The seller may request no escalations, make your best offer or you may decide not to include an escalation and just make your best offer. There can be a downside to including an escalation addendum and your agent should review that with you according to your offer situation.

8. Do not include a three day neighborhood review contingency. This tightens up the timeline in the seller's mind. Obviously, review the area first.

9. Sign off on the seller disclosure statement (if it is properly filled out) such that you waive your right to terminate your deal based on a three day review of it.

10. When appropriate, in addition to the cover letter your agent should be writing, you may also write a personalized letter to the seller to go with your offer. You agent can advise when this might be helpful and can help you craft the letter so it is complimentary but not over the top rainbows and unicorns.

Earnest Money Deposit...

What is an Earnest Money Deposit (EMD)? An EMD is the amount of money you tender and pledge such that if you do not fulfill your end of the contract and pull out of the deal for no legal reason, then the seller is going to keep a portion or all of your EMD as compensation for wasting their time. In reality, the EMD is somewhat of a formality and it is pretty hard to lose it unless you just flake out on the deal for no legal reason and there are no more contingencies left to legally terminate your deal.

It appears that earnest money deposits came into play during 1980s. Prior to the EMD being used, buyers would sometimes write up offers simultaneously on several houses and then make up their mind as to which one they wanted later. So they would get three offers accepted and then later on back out of the other two deals. This was unfair to sellers and using an EMD with each offer helped to stop this. The EMD was created most likely by a savvy buyer's agent who wanted the sellers to take his buyer's offer seriously. So they pledged a certain amount of money to show their offer was "earnest" not a frivolous offer that could easily be withdrawn on whim. EMD took off and to my knowledge most residential transactions in the United States have some form of EMD involved. Where I practice, it is expected and if your agent submits your offer without an earnest money promissory note or a copy of your EMD check attached, you can count on any smart listing agent advising the seller not to consider your offer until that is taken care of.

Traditionally when you meet to write up your offer you are most likely going to need your check book. Remember what checks are? We don't use them very much anymore but in this case you will more than likely need a hard copy check. I have taken a few clients to the bank to introduce them to checks. Yes, there is a generation that does not use checks or seemingly knows about them. You and your real estate agent should have discussed in your initial meeting the approximate amount you will need to have available in your checking account to cover your earnest money deposit. I feel safe in saying it will most likely be a $1,000 or more. The old school "rule" in the Seattle metro area was that the expected earnest money deposit was typically three percent of the list price. It got as high as five percent during the boom for certain areas.

Bring your check book when you write up your offer and you will make the check out to either the escrow company you are choosing to use or to the agent's brokerage. It depends on what the specific rules are at your agent's brokerage as to how they will want this check made out. Do not make the check out to "cash" or to your agent's name, the listing agent's name or the seller's name! Your agent should then make a photo copy of your check and will then hopefully white out the routing number on the bottom of the photocopied check, which helps mitigate the potential for fraud. Then a copy of your EMD check will be submitted with your offer. This has been the traditional way of handling the EMD. In the past, any serious listing agent required a EMD check copy with an offer before she would recommend that her seller review the offer.

However, today many buyers and agents are now meeting online to write up the offer, via an electronic signature verification service which some MLS and state laws now accept as okay for real estate transactions (verify this for your state). In Washington State via the NWMLS, this service is Authentisign. I think meeting online and using electronic signatures is a great tool, especially in the counter offer phase. If you are going to write up/sign your offer online (not meet in person with your agent) then how will your agent get your EMD check copy to present with your offer?

In this case, your agent will most likely use an Earnest Money Promissory Note Form 31 (in WA State). This note binds you to make the agreed upon earnest money deposit at a later date. It is a legal substitute for the check's hard copy is one way of looking at it. Many agents who meet with their clients in person to write up an offer are now using the earnest money promissory note instead of collecting your hard copy EMD check right away. There are now stricter laws in play (in WA State) as to who has to hold the EMD check, how long before it has to be delivered to escrow or the brokerage and deposited. Thus, some agents and brokerages now prefer that you the buyer write out and deliver the EMD check directly to escrow yourself. Regardless of what rules and norms are in play where you live, remember that you need to have the earnest money deposit funds on hand in your checking account before you write out the check or fill out the earnest money promissory note.

Common sense, when it is more of a buyer's market then the EMD amount usually diminishes. When it is a seller's market, or a multiple offer situation, the EMD typically increases. It is really purely psychological but that is how the game is usually played. You and your loan person should discuss the EMD's approximate amount and she can advise you if you can have that money gifted to you by a relative or not. More important, if you are getting funds gifted to you, what kind of written documentation for those gift funds is the underwriter going to require? If you are going to cash out a CD or get the EMD from your retirement account (what's left of it), please make sure you do this before you start touring properties. I could write pages on the bureaucratic tangles and delays with buyer's funds not properly releasing or transferring to their checking account. It is best to get that taken care of up front to avoid any potential drama.

The EMD you provide is letting the seller know you are serious (earnest) about this offer. When the EMD is delivered, per the terms of the purchase and sale agreement, to the designated escrow office (more on escrow later), then escrow cashes it and holds it until your settlement/closing goes through. You and your loan person will decide how the EMD gets applied. It could go towards your purchase price, your down payment, or towards your closing costs and pre-paid items. Sometimes you do actually get it refunded at closing if it is not needed for those items. If your EMD is used in the transaction, then it will appear as a line item on your settlement statement and you will see how it is applied at your signing appointment (more later).

If you legally terminate your deal, per the stated terms in the purchase and sale agreement, and your agent files the appropriate paperwork then you will get your EMD refunded. Escrow will require certain signed forms from both parties be submitted first before they will write a check and refund your EMD. One of the most common ways to get your EMD back is if you do your inspection and discover that there are way more issues with this house than you bargained for. Your agent would submit the 35R (Inspection Response Form in WA State) and your EMD would be refunded if the 35R is filed properly and on time. So you do your inspection, get freaked, decide to get out of the deal, file the appropriate forms within the specified time frame, and get your EMD back. If you are working with a competent agent who is organized and you follow his advice regarding deadlines, filing forms, then you should not stress too much about potentially losing your EMD. For what it is worth, I have never had a client lose an EMD and from what I have heard others in this industry say, it is fairly hard to outright lose/forfeit your EMD. But again, working with someone who is up on things and truly knows the forms and what they are doing is important.

Seller Disclosure...

In Washington State, a Seller Disclosure Statement, Form 17, is usually provided by the seller (most states have or require a similar seller disclosure statement, check to see what is required in your state). A good listing agent will have this form posted with the listing on the MLS and your agent can forward it to you. I think it is wise, whenever possible, for a buyer to review the seller disclosure statement prior to writing up their offer, certainly before their inspection. When this form is not posted online, I always ask the listing agent to send it over. Sometimes they will not respond, and other times they may say the seller has not filled it out yet. I always find that strange, especially if the property has been on the market for a few days or more. Why hasn't the seller filled out this form yet, are they trying to hide something? Is the listing agent forgetful and did not remember to have the seller fill it out, what's the story? This form is currently five pages long (in WA State) and it has questions about the condition of the property, environmental questions, age of property, etc.... The seller has the option of answering *"yes, no, don't know."* If they answer yes to any question that has an asterisk, then a written explanation needs to be provided.

As a buyer's agent, I can tell you this form is almost always an issue. It is either not prepared so it cannot be reviewed in advance or it is filled out incorrectly; seller signature, initials are missing, questions are skipped that need to be answered, no written explanation provided where required, an out-of-date version of the form has been used, etc.... I never advise my buyer sign off on this form until it is completed in full by the seller on the most recent version. Usually I have to send back a list of items to the listing agent asking them to have the seller correct/answer or have them fill out the most current version of this form. Here is a **tip**, if you get a seller disclosure statement and it is completely filled out and has detailed written explanations where required and maybe even some additional repair information attached to it, that could actually be a good sign. A seller that is that thorough is probably someone who has stayed on top of things in terms of maintaining their home.

In WA State, the buyer can sign off on the seller disclosure statement such that they have waived their right to terminate the deal based on receipt of this seller disclosure review. Or they can sign such that they then have three days, after receipt, to review the seller disclosure, ask questions and terminate the deal based on not liking what they find in the disclosure. I would not advise a buyer sign off such that the disclosure statement review period is waived upon receipt, unless it is a multiple offer scenario. Why not give yourself an additional way to terminate your deal, via the three day review period?

Please note that the information provided here for the seller disclosure statement is related to WA State practices. Your state may handle this statement differently or have different laws/requirements. There are times when you are not going to receive a Seller Disclosure Statement, Form 17. One would be if the property is an estate sale. Fran's mother owned and lived in the house and she passed away. Fran inherited her mother's house. Fran, the estate, is not required to provide a seller disclosure statement to a buyer. Foreclosure sales (bank owned properties) are not going to provide a seller disclosure statement. For a while, new construction developers were not filling out the standard seller disclosure statement but were incorporating it (or a version of it) in their required builder addendum forms. Now, most new construction projects are providing the standard seller disclosure statement and are no longer incorporating them in their builder addendums.

Sometime a listing agent will say that the seller disclosure statement is not being provided because his seller is selling the property "*as is.*" That holds no legal merit. "*As is*" does not magically remove a seller's liability or their obligation to provide a seller disclosure statement when required. Other times a landlord seller, who rents out a property but has never lived in it, will say they are not required to provide a buyer with a seller disclosure statement. That is not true as landlords are required to provide them, regardless if they have ever personally occupied the property or not.

Please note, if a seller does not provide a seller disclosure statement and is legally required to do so, then you as a buyer most likely have a legal right to terminate your deal all the way up until closing and have your earnest money deposit refunded. This is a situation that does sometimes occur and in this case a local real estate attorney will advise you on how to proceed. However, common sense indicates if a seller is dragging their feet on providing you with this form, then what are they hiding, what's the issue? I would personally move on and either not offer on the property or terminate and move on. Another red flag is when a seller completes the seller disclosure statement but answers "*don't know*" to every question or the majority of questions. Why is that, are they really that clueless about their property?

Important to note, the seller disclosure statement is usually not part of the purchase and sale agreement. It is a form that Washington State law requires most residential property sellers to fill out and provide to a buyer. There is no due date or rule that a seller should have this filled out when they list. Again, you could not receive this form all the way up until the day before closing and if you sign off on it, still close on time. However, I would want to see the seller disclosure form long before closing day is nearing. I always advise sellers that I work with to complete this seller disclosure statement prior to the listing going live and answer every question truthfully and to their best ability. If a buyer or seller has content related questions about this form, they need to consult with a local real estate attorney for help. A real estate agent is not allowed to provide help with answering or interpreting the contents/answers provided on this form. The buyer's agent can check to make sure the most current version of this form has been provided and all applicable questions are answered, explanations provided if required, and all pages are properly signed/initialed by the seller. That's it; anything else requires assistance from a real estate attorney.

This does not sound like rocket science does it? I could rant for pages as to how frustrating this form can be when I am a buyer's agent. Please keep in mind, that the seller disclosure statement is not a guarantee that you then know all the problems/issues a property may have. It is merely a jumping off point. This is a good form to have the inspector you hire review prior to doing your inspection. But still there is no guarantee that all is going to be perfect if the seller disclosure form looks okay.

Legal Description...

The final piece of paper you should acknowledge when writing up your offer (in WA State) is the legal description. Some states have forms that require this description be directly entered into the purchase and sale agreement, while others do not require a legal description at all in order to reach mutual acceptance. The legal description is usually a short paragraph provided by the title company which describes the property, "*Baylor Division, subplot two, lot six, block three of parcel seven-A of the Atkins Addition, etc....*" a real stimulating read! In Washington State, in order for an offer to technically be mutually agreed upon, the legal description must be acknowledged (initialed) by both the seller and the buyer. A good listing agent will have ordered preliminary title when she takes a listing and the title company will provide her with the legal description for the property. She will have had her sellers initial it and hopefully has posted the legal description with her listing on the MLS when the listing goes live. There have been incidents where the seller did not provide a legal description and/or only one side acknowledged it. This technically leaves a legal gap and one could argue that failure to obtain a mutually acknowledged legal description means mutual acceptance did not occur. So it is very important that the legal description be mutually signed around with the offer forms. If you live in another state, check to see what the rules are there regarding the legal description.

All Cash and 22EF...

If you are so fortunate to be flush with lots of cash and have decided you want to pay all cash for the property you are purchasing, then obviously you are not going to have your offer be contingent on financing. However, you will need to provide evidence of funds, funds availability, to the seller when you make your offer. To do this, you can have your fund's availability letter that your agent has on file updated such that it is specific to your offer price. Your agent can also use (in WA State) the 22EF Evidence of Funds Addendum with your offer. This form spells out timelines for you to provide the above mentioned funds availability letter. Also, it is used if you are paying all cash via a gift or from the proceeds you will have from the sale of a property you currently own and are selling.

You may also see this form 22EF required with a savvy listing agent, who wants you to verify any non-contingent funds (i.e. your down payment) if you are making an offer that is not all cash. The loan pre-approval letter is verifying that a loan person has reviewed a buyer's situation and has pre-approved them for a loan of X amount. This letter does not state that the loan person has verified that the buyer has the necessary cash available to pay for her down payment. Non-contingent funds would most likely be the down payment. So in an offer, the financing contingency form states the buyer is doing a conventional first mortgage and the pre-approval letter verifies this. The financing contingency form also shows the buyer is doing a 20% down payment. That 20% has most likely not been verified by the lender and certainly the lender's pre-approval letter does not state it has.

Therefore, the buyer needs to have that 20% available in cash in a savings account, investment account, a gift from someone, etc.... This all needs to be verified up front. Hence, smart listing agents are now requiring buyers submit the 22EF form with their offer and with that form submit proof verifying funds are available to cover the down payment or other non-contingent funds that are required to close the deal. Usually a buyer will submit a copy of their most recent savings account statement and hopefully their agent will white out their account number (for fraud protection). But the buyer's name, financial institution and date of the statement should be visible and of course the required amount of money to complete the deal should show as on deposit and available for use.

Updated Pre-Approval Letter...

If you are making an offer contingent upon financing, then your agent should already have your pre-approval certificate/letter on file from when you first started your search. This form will need to be updated by your loan person when you write your offer up. Why? Let's say you are pre-approved for a loan for $300,000 and that is what your pre-approval certificate states. You decided your price cap for searching would be $280,000. You have now found a house you want to make an offer on and have decided your offer price is going to be $275,000. This offer amount of $275,000 is what your updated pre-approval certificate/letter from you loan person needs to state. This updated loan approval certificate/letter goes with your offer, as any smart seller is going to want to see this when they review your offer. Your original pre-approval certificate/letter states you are pre-approved for $300,000 and you certainly do not want the seller to have that information; i.e. then they know exactly how high you can go. So the updated pre-approval letter that goes with your offer states your offer price of $275,000. Listing agents are more inclined these days to then contact the loan person that prepares your loan pre-approval certificate/letter and check in with them, make sure all is legitimate and ask any questions the seller may have about your financing. Your loan person should not give away private information about you or let the listing agent/seller know how high your total pre-approval amount is.

A few years back I was the listing agent and a buyer submitted an offer on my seller's house. Their agent had most of the offer paperwork filled out correctly but they submitted the buyer's original pre-approval letter that was a two months old. It clearly stated the buyer was pre-approved for a $425,000 loan and that was not based on the seller paying any allowable closing costs or pre-paid items for the buyer. The list price of my client's house was $375,000 and the buyer's offer price was $368,000 with the buyer asking the seller to pay their closing costs of something like $4,500. Had their loan person updated their pre-approval letter and their agent submitted their offer with the offer specific loan pre-approval letter, we would have had no clue that the buyer's pre-approval was for over $368,000 and that the buyer's pre-approval was not contingent upon the seller paying for the buyer's pre-paid items and closing costs. Thanks to their lack of attention to detail, my seller knew the buyer's hand. Thus, the seller countered back at full list price with the seller not paying any of the buyer's closing costs. The buyer accepted that counter offer. I never figured out if the buyer had any clue that the un-updated, loan pre-approval letter submitted with his offer gave his hand away. Unfortunately, based on the stories I hear, this kind of sloppy work is not that uncommon.

Does Not Convey...

Another item your agent should keep you apprised of when you are touring and certainly when you are writing up your offer are any items at the property that do not convey. When a listing agent takes a listing he will hopefully ask the sellers if there is anything they intend to take with them (besides their personal belongings) when they move. The sellers might say they are taking the dining room chandelier or the gnome statues in the back yard.

The chandelier is an attached item and would not be considered personal property. Personal property is usually defined as anything that is not affixed to the land; movable property. Your lender is not going to allow your mortgage to include personal property. Prior to taking a listing a good listing agent will first try and convince the seller to go ahead and replace the chandelier. As in remove the chandelier they intend to take and buy and install another one. This keeps things very simple and no one gets fixated on the chandelier (yes there have been stubborn deals where each side demanded the chandelier or the deal was off). However, some sellers will not agree to replace the chandelier prior to listing. So, their listing agent should make a note in the listing report that the chandelier, *"does not convey"* or *"is not included"* or *"sellers are keeping the dining room chandelier,"* etc.... A smart listing agent is going to also insist that the seller hang a sign from the chandelier noting once again this item stays with the seller. A good buyer's agent will note in his client's offer that the dining room chandelier is going to be removed and remain with the seller. The buyer's agent may write in that the seller agrees to replace said chandelier with one of equal style/value or seller to install a specific chandelier the buyer wants, including the name and model number of the buyer's preferred chandelier.

Those Pesky Gnomes...

The garden gnome statues are another matter. Technically they are considered personal property as they are not permanently attached to the house or land. There have been many a hissy fit over missing yard gnomes! A good buyer's agent is going to remind you in advance when you are touring that the yard gnomes will be removed as they are personal property. Other examples of seller's personal property that is usually outdoors are: birdbaths, portable storage sheds or play houses that are not permanently attached to the land via a slab foundation, firewood, moveable outdoor grills, any potted plants, swing sets or play equipment unless they are installed in-ground via cement. If the garden gnome statues are left by the seller, well then you win the gnome statue lottery! Otherwise, count on the seller taking them.

Appliances...

The purchase and sale agreement has boxes (in WA State) to check off for appliances that are included in the sale of the property. The listing report should clearly indicate for your agent and you as to what appliances are included with the sale and which ones are excluded. In this case, lenders do not freak out because a refrigerator or dryer is checked off as included in the sale. Yes, appliances mostly fall under the category of personal property as they can be removed (are not usually permanently attached) but lenders make an exception in this case unlike the motor boat in the forthcoming example. So appliances are items that the seller can decide to take and sometimes you will see a listing where only the stove/range is being left. The rest of the appliances are being removed by the seller. This practice of the seller taking some or all of the appliances with them when they move is more common in some states than others. Per your specific loan type and any applicable regional or county appraisal rules for say FHA loans, lenders are going to usually require there be an operational stove/range and kitchen sink in order for the property to pass appraisal.

Real Property Only...

When you write up your offer for a property only the actual real property (the land/structures that are attached) should be included with the exception of the boxes or blanks your agent fills in to indicate any appliances that are included with the sale. Your agent should not include in your offer an itemized list of personal items you wish to purchase from the seller. For example, a listing agent may advertise that included in the sale of the lake house is the owner's motor boat or worse yet, "*Free motor boat with full price offer.*" The lake house and land are what your lender is loaning you money to purchase and what the purchase and sale agreement covers. The motor boat is considered personal property belonging to the seller. It should not be included in your offer. How would this work then?

You would have your agent write up your offer for the lake house and your lender will approve it and lend you money for that purchase. As a separate agreement, apart from your purchase of the lake house, you and the seller can come to terms on your own regarding the motor boat. A buyer's agent should not write in your purchase and sale agreement that the seller agrees to leave the motor boat. Agents are supposed to use the MLS forms to facilitate the transfer of real property. In addition, including personal property in your purchase and sale agreement will upset the lender, they view that as a monetary gain for you and they are not lending you money to purchase personal items (again the one exception to this are any included appliances). A lender will consider the motor boat as a monetary gain, an increase in your assets. Thus, if you want the motor boat you would want to create your own private agreement (or have an attorney do this) where you and the seller work out the ownership of the motor boat. As you can see this can be confusing. In this case, the listing agent could mention that the motor boat is an item the seller is willing to privately negotiate with the buyer. The motor boat technically should not be included in the listing as a buyer bonus because a lender will not allow it and in some states, including the motor boat (personal property) in the listing verbiage, especially as an incentive for a full list price offer, is a violation of MLS rules.

Another way this comes up is you tour a property and there is a list of the seller's furnishings that are for sale. The seller says a buyer can purchase the dining room set for $1,500. If you want the dining room set, you should make your offer for the house and get that agreed to and then you and the seller work out the purchase of the dining room set on your own. Your offer should not state something like, "*$320,000 purchase price including the seller's dining room set.*" or include verbiage on an addendum, "*Seller agrees to leave dining room set upon receipt of $1,500 from buyer at or on closing.*"

What about the listing that states the offer price is $400,000 vacant or $430,000 including furnishings? Again, those personal items, "furnishings" need to be negotiated and paid for own your own, without your real estate agent's involvement. A lender is not going to allow your mortgage to include $30,000 for furnishings. You would make an offer for the vacant property and then broker the sale of the furnishings separately. Here is a **tip**, if you are buying a furnished house, make sure you include a complete itemized and visual list of all included furnishing in the transfer of personal property agreement that you and the seller sign. You should have a local real estate attorney assist you with this transfer of personal property agreement and help facilitate the verification of furnishings and payment.

One last point, what if the seller at some point after mutual agreement asks if you would like for them to leave the sofa? They are not selling the sofa to you; they are leaving it in the house if you want it. You can state you do not want the sofa and in that case the seller needs to remove it. If you do want the sofa (it is being left by the seller not sold to you) then you can say yes, please leave it. However, note that technically that is just a verbal agreement for the seller to leave the sofa for you free of charge. There is no legal obligation for the seller to actually follow through and leave the free sofa. So know if on closing you unlock the house and the sofa the seller said they were going to leave for you is not there, then that is your tough luck. Remember, your real estate agent has no part or control in this matter, so do not blame them if the seller does not leave the free sofa as promised. If the free sofa is really important to you, then you should have a written agreement that both you and the seller sign on your own stating the seller is going to leave you the sofa free of charge.

This all might sound petty and trivial, welcome to the wonderful world of residential real estate! The devil is literally in the details. Therefore, keep it simple and do not mix real property and personal property transactions and if in doubt spell it all out in writing with a local real estate attorney's help.

Real Life…

I had a buyer who was purchasing an upscale house that came with a custom designed kitchen. In the kitchen were custom cabinetry, a high end refrigerator that cost more than some people earn in a year and ditto for the restaurant grade range and oven. There were no notices posted at the house or anywhere in the listing paper work to indicate that the seller intended to take the appliances or replace them prior to moving out. The listing report indicated all of the appliances were included in the sale and that is what the purchase and sale agreement stated. Five days prior to closing, per the terms of the purchase and sale agreement, my client and I toured the house for his final walk through. The seller had already moved out and all was looking spic and span until we walked into the kitchen. The pricey refrigerator had been removed and in its place was a basic white refrigerator from Home Depot. Not only that, but this refrigerator did not fit flush within the custom designed cabinetry as the previous high end refrigerator had. Next, the million dollar range/oven was missing and a standard, four-burner, range/oven from Home Depot sat in its place. This too was dwarfed by empty space around it as the expensive range had at least eight burners and a grill and was considerably larger.

We took pictures and I immediately contacted the listing agent and escrow. The listing agent insisted that her seller was within his rights to remove the included appliances. She said the seller had replaced them with a like kind so everything was fine. I then contacted the listing agent's designated broker to let him know there was a problem. I sent over photos of the appliances that were currently in the kitchen and suggested they compare that with the photos of the kitchen's appliances that were posted with the listing online. After many calls, their stance was that the seller felt he was within his rights to remove the refrigerator and range/oven and felt his replacements were acceptable. I advised my client postpone his signing appointment and consult with a real estate attorney.

In the end, the seller had to restore the original appliances and allow us to re-inspect and then proceed to closing. Apparently the seller was furious with the listing agent for not informing him that he could not remove the appliances and replace them with cheaper substitutes. Even if he had replaced them with similar grade/style appliances, my buyer could have probably gone after him to put the original appliances back in the kitchen. If the seller had indicated per the listing paperwork and via the mutually signed purchase and sale agreement that the refrigerator and range/oven were not included with the sale, then this would have been a different situation. It is frequently the details in real estate that make or break a smooth sale. In this case, the listing agent could have been clearer with her seller as to what he agreed to, via the listing paperwork and the signed around purchase and sale agreement. It meant he could not remove or replace the refrigerator or range. Still, there are cases where the listing agent is clear with her client, and the seller still decides to up and change the rules and terms without notifying anyone. Always something!

SIX

MUTUAL AGREEMENT

Seller Response...

Once you have submitted your offer, the seller then has a specified time period to review it and respond. The seller's review time period is usually stated on the first page of the offer and indicated as "Offer Expiration." Typically 9 p.m. (on the indicated offer expiration date) is when your offer is no longer valid. The seller can do one of the following when they receive your offer.

1. Ignore your offer and never respond (technically they can't ignore it if it is full price and follows all of the stated terms in the posted listing)
2. Counter your offer
3. Accept your offer.

If you make a low-ball offer and the seller is highly insulted, they could very well just ignore your offer and not bother to respond. Thus the offer expires and their non-response is your response. The seller can accept your offer completely as is, making no changes at all to any of the stated terms and in that case you have mutual agreement. Mutual agreement means all parties have agreed to and acknowledged the stated terms of the agreement and now the timelines and contingencies in the deal begin.

Any substantive change that a seller makes to the offer you submit is considered a counter offer. You then have a review period to respond to the seller's counter offer or to let it pass and thus the game ends. All changes on the offer paperwork should be acknowledged by both parties with their initials/dates. Including a date with all initialed changes may not always be legally necessary but to keep things clear and for best practice, a good agent is going to insist you date everything you sign or initial.

If something changed needs to be written out, it should be executed on a blank addendum or a counter offer form so that it is legible and clear to all parties before they acknowledge it. There is nothing more unprofessional and potentially confusing than when a seller or their agent hand scribbles in a change and submits that to you as a counter offer; especially in today's world where online forms, online signings are accessible and easy to do. Keep it simple, keep it clear, and make it concise. If you do not understand a seller's counter offer, then it is probably best to have a real estate attorney explain it to you and/or revise the wording such that it is clear and legal. Your agent can execute very simple counter offer verbiage or repair requests but if it begins to get complex or legal in any manner, it is best to have a local real estate attorney advise how you should word it. Your agent is not a real estate attorney and cannot practice law via your offer form's verbiage.

Let's say you and a seller are going back and forth on the agreed upon sale price with counter offers. At no point do you have mutual agreement until all of the terms are mutually agreed upon and acknowledged. Therefore, during the counter offer back and forth the seller could accept another offer. That sometimes happens and that is why in real estate, time really is of the essence. Your agent needs to be organized, timely, and available. He needs to know how to keep a paper trail of when your offer, counter offers are submitted, accepted or rejected. It can backfire on you big time, if your agent does not understand the importance of filing the paperwork and properly documenting it. Once your offer is mutually accepted, the listing agent should change the status of the property in the MLS. It could go from active status to pending inspection or pending. The seller still may wish to take a back-up offer but that does not impact you except that you know there is a back-up offer from another buyer should you decide to terminate this deal or your loan does not go through.

If for some reason you decide after you submit your offer and are awaiting the seller's response that you no longer want to buy the property, your agent should fill out a Withdrawal of Offer or Counter Offer Form 36A (in WA State) and submit that to the listing agent. Failing that, if the seller accepted your offer with no changes before you submitted your offer rescission form, technically you would have mutual agreement. That said you will most likely have a number of contingencies in your deal which would allow you to get out of the deal, without losing your earnest money deposit, the most common being your inspection contingency.

Once you have reached mutual agreement (both parties have agreed to and acknowledged via their signatures all of the terms in the offer paperwork), your contingency timelines come in to play. I provide my clients with an easy to follow timeline sheet that outlines when the specific contingencies in their deal expire, when certain tasks need to be completed, and important dates and deadlines to be aware of. I usually provide this sheet to the client's loan person and to escrow if they are interested. This way everyone knows at a quick glance when a specific deadline is for your transaction.

Inspection...

Hopefully you see the value in having a licensed inspector look at your property and so the Inspection Contingency Form 35 (in WA State) has been included as part of your offer. The norm for a residential inspection time period is usually five to seven days, sometimes the seller will agree to 10 days. Usually the inspection time period is fairly short, because the seller does not want to tie their property up too long, via your inspection contingency. You might do your inspection and decide to terminate the deal and move on. From the seller's perspective, they want to know sooner, rather than later if you are going to proceed with the transaction. Getting the inspection contingency out of the way is one of the best indicators the seller has that you are moving forward with the deal.

Also, your lender is not going to want to wait forever to hear back about whether or not your inspection is complete and you are moving ahead with the deal. They have a lot of work to do on their end. They usually want to hold off on ordering the appraisal (more on that later) for the property until they know your inspection contingency is satisfied. You will most likely be on the hamster wheel about the house, and the sooner you can get your inspection done and know more about the property's condition the better you are going to feel. Even if you have 10 days to do your inspection, I always advise getting your inspection(s) done sooner rather than later, usually within a day or two of mutual agreement if possible.

When you first meet with your agent, hopefully included in their buyer packet will be a list of at least three inspector's names that you may wish to investigate. You can also ask around and see what inspectors any friends or coworkers may have used. In Washington State, all home inspectors must be licensed and you are required to receive an Inspector Referral Disclosure Form 41-D which lists any home inspectors your agent is either related to or who have been hired by the agent to inspect a property the agent is personally purchasing. I advise first investigating inspectors when you start your home buying process. Get information and come up with a short list of inspectors you might want to use. Once you have made an offer and it is accepted, then you will want to choose the best inspector for the property and your criteria. You may want to ask an inspector questions before you decide to use them.

Questions to Ask an Inspector...

Here is a brief list of questions you may want to ask a home inspector prior to hiring them.

1. How many years have you been doing home inspections?
2. Are you a licensed inspector in this state? (some states require they be, others do not)
3. What did you do prior to becoming a home inspector?
4. Is home inspecting your full time job?
5. What does your inspection typically cover?
6. What does your inspection exclude?

7. Do you have errors and omissions insurance?

8. Do you check all appliances that are included in the sale?

9. Do you check crawl spaces, attics?

10. Can you point out to me the water main shut off valve when you do your inspection?

11. Do you check for insects and rodents?

12. When do you provide a written narrative report to your clients? Do you also provide a copy of this report to my agent?

13. Will you complete a HUD inspection form or other form my lender may require be completed by my home inspector in order to complete my loan? If so, do you charge extra for this?

14. Are you available for questions from me, my agent, my loan person?

15. Will you advise me as to how much certain repairs will cost? (a good inspector will <u>not</u> do that)

16. How much do you charge (they'll need to know the size of the house)?

17. How long do you think this inspection will take, one hour, two hours, etc…?

18. What is your preferred method of payment?

19. Are you currently a member of the American Society of Home Inspectors (ASHI)?

You will want to mention any special issues with the house that may be of concern to you, see if they are able to evaluate or provide insight on those items. At a minimum, you are hiring a general inspector who can give you an overview of things. No general inspector I have come across is going to check out the internet connection, phone service, check the sewer lines, etc.... They are there to take a look at what is visible and accessible. A good inspector will not reel off repair costs for items as he inspects things. Legally, he should not be doing that and it is best for you to verify on your own what certain repair items' average costs are by contacting a few, local contractors for general estimates. This is where I advise all of my buyers to come up with a five year improvement plan for the property they are purchasing. What kind of annual maintenance budget should be factored in for the property and what special remodeling projects do you want to do down the road?

Any item of concern that falls into a more specialized category is going to require a specialized inspector. For example, if you are buying an older house and you are concerned about whether or not the sewage line from the house to the street is clear and connected, then you would want to hire a company that scopes sewage lines. They can provide you with a report as to the condition of the line. Sometimes, your general inspector may recommend in his report that you have a specialist evaluate something. Such as, the electrical panel box appears to have some issues; the inspector will then recommend it be evaluated by a licensed electrician. If you want to pursue that, then your agent will give notice of an additional inspection, based on your primary inspector's report. Per the terms of your inspection contingency, you will hire the specialist inspector to come out and evaluate what needs to be looked at. This agreed upon additional inspection timeline is typically very short, so you will have to move quickly to have this additional inspection completed within the timeline.

Your agent is not an inspector but if your agent suggests you consider hiring an additional specialist inspector, then you would be best served to try and get them to all come out and do their work on one date and time. For example, it is obvious to your agent and you that the house you are looking at appears to have some electrical issues. It is almost a given that your general inspector is going to recommend having a licensed electrician evaluate things, thus an additional inspection. So you know in advance to go ahead and hire a general inspector and find a licensed electrician and pay to have them both come out on the same date/time slot (preferably) and do their inspections. This is also true if you know you want to have the sewer line scoped, etc.... All of my buyers have at least one inspection. The most inspections a client of mine has done on a property is seven. These folks had very deep pockets and very deep neurosis! Coordinating seven different inspectors converging on one house on one day and one general time frame was like herding cattle. But all worked out fine, my clients felt better and were happy.

Your inspection date is also a great time to have your decorator, remodeling contractor, in-laws, children come along and check things out. A **tip**, test your cell phone reception at the property while your inspection is being done. You also might have a special situation like one of my client's did a while back. He was a recording artist and planned to convert the basement of the house into his recording studio. He happened to casually mention that he hoped his equipment would work in the basement, that the pipes or whatever would not create some kind of feedback. I immediately told him to bring some of his recording equipment to his inspection appointment, set it up in the basement and test it out. He was a bit taken aback but when I pointed out how he might not end up liking the house if his recording studio did not work, he agreed. Turns out all was good when he tested his equipment and today his home based recording business is booming.

Your agent's role in your inspection is to notify the listing agent as to the time and date you will be doing your inspection. Then your agent needs to show up, let you and your posse of people into the property and remain there for the duration of your inspection. Your agent is there to make sure you and your posse do not break or steal anything. They are not there to assist with the inspection or inspect any condition for you. Your agent should never leave you and your inspector alone at the property while she runs out to do errands, goes for coffee. That is against the law. Your agent can duck out if she has a licensed assistant or another licensed agent remain there with you at the property while she is gone. This might be one reason why some agents don't like for you to do an inspection because it takes up their time and inspections are typically fairly boring for a buyer's agent.

Also, remember when you set up your appointment with your inspector to run that appointment's date and time by your agent first. He will need to make sure he is available and he needs to verify with the listing agent that this date/time is okay with the seller. Legally, your agent should not be making the inspection appointment for you or paying for it. This is a contractor you are hiring to do work for you and you need to independently find them, book them, and pay for them. If someone else pays for your inspection there could be a legal gray zone as to who the inspection was really done for, who the inspector legally has to answer to. So avoid all of those possible issues and contract/pay for it yourself.

Another **tip** I give to my clients, if you have a friend or relative who has been involved in construction or home repair work for many years, see if you can entice them (via lunch, donuts) to attend your inspection with you. They are not a licensed inspector and cannot provide you with your written report but they are another knowledgeable pair of eyes that can look at things with you and your inspector.

A typical inspection takes between one and two hours (longer if it is a larger property) and it is best to do it in day light hours if possible. You need to be present for the inspection or appoint someone to represent you. I strongly suggest you attend your inspection. You would never appoint your agent to represent you in your absence at the inspection; a friend or other third party is a much better choice. No agent who has a clue about liability issues is going to agree to represent you in your absence at your inspection. This is the most expensive item (or close to it) that you will purchase, it makes good sense for you to make sure you do an inspection and that you are there during your inspection. I've literally met with a client's boss in order to help them get time off from work so they can be present for their inspection. Anyone who has bought a house knows how important the inspection is. If someone's boss is cranky about letting them have time off in the day to attend their inspection, then their next big move should be finding a new job/boss, but only after closing!

You need to realize that even if you have the property inspected by 100 different inspectors things still can and do go wrong later when you own the house, condo, vacant land, etc.… There is always risk involved when buying. No inspection can possibly guarantee that everything is okay. Sometimes there can be a problem down the road with a property that is not anyone's fault, it just exists and it is now on your shift to address it and pay for it. If this is not something you can be comfortable with, then renting is most likely your best option.

Never allow an agent or loan person to talk you into forging an inspection report or an inspector invoice/receipt. This is completely illegal and if you are party to this, you have at a minimum committed loan fraud which tends to fall into the felony category of crimes. Not something you want to be involved with and certainly not something in your best interest. This does happen, as I have heard firsthand in my classes and you do not want to be involved in anything like this.

One last item, sometimes the listing agent will promote that the seller had the house inspected when they purchased or right before they listed it and give you a copy of the seller's inspection report. That's great, have a look at it and take it with a grain of salt. It does not mean that you should not pay for your own inspection and thoroughly inspect the property. If you are purchasing with financing, your loan person is going to require you do an inspection and they will not (or should not) accept the seller's inspection report, no matter how recent it is. In my opinion, you know you are working with an unethical agent if she tries to talk you into forgoing your own inspection based on the inspection report the seller has provided. I heard a story where a buyer's agent did this and got the buyer to tell their lender that they had the property inspected and then submitted an altered copy of the seller's inspection report to the lender as proof. Again, please do not get involved in this type of scenario, it is illegal and not in your best interest!

A Good Inspector...

It is important that you find an inspector who is experienced, who can address issues you may have with a particular property and most important is neutral and factual based. Please avoid the inspectors who have enormous egos (just like you should avoid agents/lenders with maniac size egos). There is nothing worse than when a client hires Mr. Blowhard Inspector who views his job as finding something wrong with the property and if nothing is of major concern still casts doubt nonetheless. These inspector types like to crow about how much they know, show off their new technology toys, and bad mouth agents and sellers non-stop. They see their role as bonding with you and bad mouthing the property and agents in order to facilitate that bond. Nothing is worse except maybe when these blowhards start telling you how expensive it is to make the repairs they think you should make and how if they were you they'd keep looking and find yourself a real deal. They will then go into their real estate spiel and try and impress you with how up on the market they are and what good sale prices are, on and on.

I say if they are so interested in the real estate market, then they should go get their real estate license and sell houses. Otherwise, an inspector should focus on what she is being hired to do, evaluate the condition of the property, not provide value or pricing opinions. A good inspector is going to provide you with facts, not opinions. You will take those facts and then determine if this is something you want to pass on, i.e. terminate your deal based on what you discovered via the facts of your inspection. Or you want to ask the seller to address some of the issues your inspector found. If only minor things were noted in the inspection, and you are okay with them, you decide to move forward, with no repair requests for the seller.

Inspection Response...

Your loan person does not usually get a complete copy of your inspection report. In Washington State, they will want the signed off Inspection Response For Form 35 (Form 35R) and sometimes they need a paid-in-full invoice from your inspector. Form 35R provides your response to the seller after you have completed your inspection (via the Inspection Contingency Form 35). You indicate one of the following on the 35R: you are okay with your inspection findings and are now waving your inspection contingency; you did not like the inspection results and are terminating your offer (requesting your earnest money deposit be returned); you are requesting repairs or modifications from the seller.

Assuming you ask for a couple of items be repaired and the seller indicates in their response portion of the 35R that they agree to take care of those items, then the 35R is signed around and the inspection contingency is satisfied. That is what your loan person wants to know and needs to have back so they can start moving your loan paperwork along. They usually will not ask questions as to what your inspector found or did not find. If you request items be repaired prior to closing, via the 35R, then your loan person is going to need written verification (via your agent or you) that those items were completed and paid for.

Occasionally, a loan person's underwriter might require a condition that was repaired be re-inspected and confirm it is now okay. An example of this would be the house's roof needs to be replaced prior to closing. Your 35R had that as a condition and the seller agreed to replace the roof. Your agent collects the roof replacement receipt, marked paid-in-full, and you all visually verify the work was done during your final walk through of the property (five days prior to closing in WA State). If the loan underwriter is picky, they may require you have your original inspector go back out and verify in writing that the roof was replaced and is now okay. You would most likely have to pay your inspector to go back out, usually for a reduced fee, but still something to be aware of. Please do not get pouty with your loan person if this occurs, as it is something that is usually completely out of their control. Underwriters are notorious for springing surprise requests on loan officers, so please have some patience if this happens.

Home Insurance...

Once your inspection is past and you know you are moving ahead and the deal is going to close, you need to make sure you get home insurance for the property. Your loan person is going to require this and your agent should remind you to go make written application for your insurance. The home insurance policy can usually be set up over the phone. They will ask questions about the property and give you a quote. You will want your home insurance policy to start on your stated closing date.

I usually include a Homeowner Insurance Addendum Form 22VV (in WA State) with my buyer's offers. This way if for some reason you cannot obtain a standard homeowners insurance policy for the property, then your agent has an easy way to terminate your deal and get your EMD back if the stated and agreed upon timelines in the insurance addendum are followed. There are cases (rare) where a buyer is not able to get a homeowner policy for the property he is buying and that is when this addendum is your friend! If you are financing your purchase and your financing contingency has not been waived, then if you cannot get insurance for the property, you can also get out of the deal based on the fact your lender is unable to lend on property that is uninsurable

If you are paying all cash, and there is no requirement from a lender that you insure your home, you obviously would still want to do so. Here is a **tip**, if you own a car and have insurance on it, see if your current car insurance carrier also does home insurance policies. It is typically less expensive if you have both your car and home insurance policies with the same company. Also, sometimes people think if they are purchasing a condo they do not have to get home insurance. Not true. Most condo associations require that you insure your unit. That would mean you insure your actual space and its contents. The association will have a master policy that insures the condo common areas, hallways, garage, grounds, etc.... With a condo, the good news is the home owner's insurance cost is very low, almost the same as renter's insurance.

Home Buyer Warranty...

Your agent hopefully made you aware of home buyer warranties and what they are when you met for your initial meeting. Usually a home buyer warranty will insure the systems in a property that you are purchasing for a set period of time after you purchase. For example, you purchase a home built in 1980 and the furnace and appliances are from that year as well. If you have a home buyer warranty policy in place, then if the furnace needs replacing or the old dish washer dies six months after you purchase, the home buyer warranty will usually cover some of the costs to replace those failed items. Different companies offer different levels of coverage, have varying lengths of time, deductibles, and price points. I advise clients to learn more about the different homebuyer warranty companies and available warranties at the start of their search. Once we identify the specific property they are interested in, then they can revisit the home buyer warranty option and decide if they think it is worthwhile purchasing one for that property or not. Sometimes sellers will offer a home buyer warranty as a buying incentive.

CHARLES CHAPLIN

Appraisal...

Once your deal is mutually accepted, your loan person should receive a complete copy of it from your real estate agent. The loan person can then start to set things up and get the ball rolling on your financing. Usually, a loan person likes to wait until your inspection contingency has been removed to order your appraisal. You have to pay for your appraisal and your loan person will let you know how much this will cost and when and how to pay for it. You and your agent do not attend the appraisal. The appraiser is an independent party contracted by your lender via a random lottery assignment system. In the past, lenders were allowed to cherry pick which appraisers they worked with and contracted to evaluate property values. This led to some cases of collusion. Thus, the laws changed and now appraisers are randomly assigned. The appraiser is trained and licensed to evaluate property and ensure that the lender is loaning money for a viable commodity (no Brooklyn Bridges or phantom homes) and that the price you are paying for the property is of fair market value. Fair market values means the sale price is congruent with other similar sales. In other words, you are not over paying (they are not over lending) for a property. In a hot and increasing market, when values of homes can literally shoot up over night, the appraiser has to be more diligent due to the rapidly accelerating market conditions. What seemed overpriced last week may now be the new going rate. The appraiser is going to visit the property and check it out in person and she is going to pull active and sold comparison reports, just like the ones you hopefully used when you determined what your offer price should be.

A few years ago a property my client was buying appeared to be in good shape but the inspector took great pains to question every single thing with this house. He then proceeded to tell her that she had paid too much for the house. On and on this went and at the end he told her she should back out of the deal and find a real bargain. A good inspector never gives real estate advice just as a good agent never gives inspection related advice. My client paid him and we both talked about it. He had put the fear of God in her about a million little items that in my opinion did not amount to much, certainly not things that would cause a serious buyer to back out of a deal.

Since she was a first time home buyer and this was her first home inspection, and she did not know what to think about what this inspector said. She really loved the house and agreed that it did not seem like something she should walk away from. She decided to hire another inspector and have her friend who works in construction attend (which I had tried to get her to do from the get go). We still had time, per the inspection contingency time period and so out to the property we went again with her new inspector. She showed him the previous inspector's report. He and her construction friend inspected the property and ripped the previous inspection report to shreds point by point. In the end, she trusted the second more neutral inspector and that report is what we worked from. She closed on the house and has never looked back.

In another transaction, I had buyers hire an inspector who I privately nick-named Andy Williams. I called him this because he appeared for the inspection wearing a v-neck cashmere sweater, expensive wool slacks and imported Italian loafers complete with tassels. Hence, he reminded me of some ancient Andy Williams TV show rerun. I thought the guy must be a decorator my clients were hiring, I was wrong. This well dressed but rude man was retired from his former career and now worked part time as a home inspector. He did not shake my hand when he arrived at the house, kept his back turned to me, and would not speak to me or acknowledge my presence throughout the inspection.

Manners and protocol aside, this guy just plain sucked. He went through the house telling my clients which walls to knock out, how to install hardwood flooring, where recessed lights would be a good idea, and how much all of this should cost. All things a good decorator would advise but not a home inspector. After an hour of this, I asked if he intended to check the included appliances, to which he coldly replied with his back to me, "*I don't check appliances.*" I advised my clients that they might want ask him to turn on the included range, the washer and dryer to make sure they were indeed operational. He just smirked. He told my clients the outlets in the house needed new covers. The cosmetic cover plates mind you, not anything inspector related like wiring or amp concerns. I asked if he would be putting on a coverall suit (to protect his fluffy clothes) and going in the crawl space under the house. That question sent Andy Williams into a complete snarl. He replied that he didn't check crawl spaces or anything that remotely involved dust or mechanics. So, what did he do, besides offer bad decorating advice? How this bozo got licensed to do home inspections is beyond me. But my clients found and chose him on their own and so I just had to smile and go along. Later, I did suggest to my clients that I thought the inspection lacked certain basic elements and asked if they would like to hire someone else to give it a whirl before their inspection contingency expired. Nope. So they closed and from what I know they are happy with their home. Here is my **tip**, if your home inspector shows up in clothes you would see Andy Williams wearing in a TV flashback episode, you might want to rethink things. In my opinion, your inspector should be getting down and dirty, literally.

SEVEN

CLOSING

Title Insurance...

Title insurance protects against future losses resulting from past events. Traditionally, the title insurance company is chosen by the seller when they list their property and the buyer then chooses an escrow company when making an offer. The seller pays for the title company to guarantee clear title so the property can be sold and the deed recorded in your name. You the buyer usually pay a title insurance premium for your lender. When a listing agent takes a listing, a good one will have a title company pull preliminary title and indicate that title company's name and the preliminary title report number in his listing. The buyer's agent then can write in that title company's name in the buyer's offer.

Whenever I run across a listing where the listing agent has not pulled preliminary title, I start to wonder what the problem is. Is there an issue with who really owns the property, is there a cloud on the title, is the listing agent completely clueless and doesn't know title needs to be pulled (not that uncommon unfortunately), etc...? Sometimes when the title company really starts to dig and verify things (after an offer is mutually accepted) they will discover hidden issues with the seller or the property, a cloud on the title that has to be cleared in order for the sale to close.

The title insurance company is going to verify the title is clear and that the person who says they are the owner is in fact legitimate and can actually sell the property you want to buy. They will verify that there are no outstanding liens, warrants, judgments against a seller. The title company will get the information they need about you from your agent or they will contact you directly. Sometimes this is where a buyer's spouse or partner's secret past comes back to haunt them. They are buying a property together and all is going well until the title company discovers there are outstanding child support payments against one of the buyers or a warrant has been issued for one of the buyers, etc.... This may come as a complete surprise to the buyer, as they have no clue a warrant was issued for them four years ago. These issues have to be successfully cleared up before the title insurance company is going to guarantee the title can be conveyed.

Your lender is going to require clear and conveyable title, via the title insurance company, before they will agree to fund your loan. This protects the lender's (and buyer's) future interest in the property. Even if you are buying all cash (no financing), you will still want title insurance. If some unknown heir of the seller suddenly pops up two years after you have closed and are the owner of the property, then the title insurance kicks in to protect you against any claim this until now unknown heir might make on the property. In essence, the title insurance for the property is primarily concerned with risk of loss from past problems that might be present when your policy is issued for the property.

The title company will send you a preliminary title commitment either by email or by snail mail and they will also being sending you updated reports as your deal progresses. You should read it over (even though it can be a bit dull) and contact the title representative with any questions you may have. The title report is going to list any known easements on the property. An easement example would be the power company's line that runs across the property you are buying. They will list the right of the power company to access the property to repair or replace the power line that runs across the property. There may be unused easements. For example, my property has a railroad easement running across the back of it. It was recorded in the late 1800s and it is unused; in fact the railroad was never built. But in theory, the railroad still has their easement/access to the back of my lot.

The title report will list your name as buyer and most likely state they are investigating to confirm you are who you say you are and not someone with outstanding warrants, judgments against you. If you have a more common name like Bob Jones, then the report will probably state there are several outstanding issues with "Bob Jones" and they are investigating. That is because your name is common and besides you, the fine upstanding citizen Bob Jones, there are others out there with the same name as you, who are trying very hard to make their appearance on *America's Most Wanted*. When buyers first see that their name needs investigating by the title company, they naturally freak. You can contact the title representative with any questions and for reassurance. You will see by the final title report that your name has been cleared and they will state there are no known issues with you.

There are also different types of title insurance and if you want to know more about the different types and what they cover and do not cover, then it is best to speak directly with the title company representative and let them fill you in on the various types, and reasons for them. Your agent should know the most common type of title insurance to indicate on your purchase and sale agreement. Sometimes there may be a question about a property line or you need to know exactly where the official property boundaries are. Your agent can request (at your expense and it is not cheap) for the title company to do an extended report. This will entail hiring a surveyor to go out and physically survey and stake the property. There are cases where I have suggested clients pay to do it and it was in their best interest to do so. Many buyers do not even glance at the title information that is sent to them but I encourage all buyers to review it and again contact the title representative directly with any title questions.

When you write up your offer, a good buyer's agent is going to include a Title Contingency Addendum Form 22T (in WA State). If filled out correctly, this addendum entitles you the buyer to review the preliminary title report for five days (usually) upon receipt. During that review time you can note any exceptions that are listed and if you give written notice of your disapproval of the exceptions noted, the seller then has a time period (usually five days) to give written notice to the buyer that they will correct all the disapproved exceptions before the closing date. If the seller does not provide written notice that they will clear the disapproved exceptions within the stated response time, then you the buyer can terminate your deal and get your earnest money deposit returned.

Another note, many times the title company has an escrow division and the listing agent will indicate the seller prefers to use the title company to also act as the escrow company for this transaction. Typically, bundling title and escrow can result in a price reduction for those services. You are only paying for your half of the escrow service but if title and escrow are bundled then your escrow fee should be discounted a bit as well. The amount you owe for escrow may be zero if the seller agrees to pay your closing costs and pre-paid items. You and your loan officer will discuss in advance how those fees are getting paid and what you are going to ask the seller to pay for. If the seller does not agree to pay any of your costs, then you and your loan officer will figure out how you are going to cover the closing costs and pre-paid items.

Escrow...

The escrow officer is a neutral third party that acts like a referee in your transaction. They work per the stated terms of your purchase and sale agreement and the lender's instructions. Escrow does not advocate for you the buyer or the seller. They are there to make sure the money in your deal is applied and disbursed properly and the deed is recorded in your name with the county recording office. The escrow officer needs to be organized, knowledgeable and able to get the deal closed. Some escrow officers are better than others. It is always completely at the client's discretion and choice which escrow company they want to use. An agent should always ask if the choice for the escrow company indicated on your offer paperwork is indeed the escrow company you wish to use. If you do not know much about escrow, then ask your agent if she has an escrow company she prefers to work with. That is no guarantee things will go smoothly but it does not hurt. The seller does not have to agree to use the escrow company you request but typically they will since they chose the title company. Occasionally there are split escrows, where the seller has one escrow company and the buyer has another escrow company. That can make things a bit more confusing but it can be done.

Your agent (if they are organized) is going to get a complete copy of your deal paperwork to escrow as soon as you have mutual agreement. Escrow will then get your information, the seller's information, and note the closing date. They will contact you at some point prior to the closing date to let you know what (if any) information they need from you. Escrow will need all of your loan documents from your loan person before they can set up your signing appointment. In some states, known as traditional closing states, you have a concurrent signing appointment and closing. Meaning, you and the seller go to the escrow office on the closing date and sign the final paperwork together and the keys are given to you then and there.

In Washington State that does not happen. It is an escrow state; there is a gap between signing and closing (usually two to three days). You will set up a signing appointment with escrow, usually a few days prior to your stated closing date. Once you have signed all of your final loan documents you are not the owner and the keys will not be given to you. The seller will have their own signing appointment but that is not your concern.

Your loan person is going to make sure that your appraisal is in and is okay. She (or her processor) will collect any other outstanding items from you and then submit all of your loan paperwork, including a copy of your signed around deal to the underwriter. The underwriter then reviews everything. They may request additional information or not. Once the loan underwriter is okay, they will release the loan documents and forward them to the escrow company. Escrow will organize all your loan documents, and prepare a settlement statement. This statement will itemize all expenses and credits for the buyer and seller on a master spreadsheet. You will only see the settlement statement for your half; you will not see the seller's information.

The escrow officer is going to have you come in for your signing appointment. If it is two of you buying together and both names are going to be on title then you both need to attend a signing appointment. If for some reason the person you are buying with is not going to be available for a signing appointment, then you will need to have a power of attorney letter drawn up in advance and notarized which gives you the legal right to sign for the other party. That can be a bit of a pain to arrange, so it is best if each person who is going to be on title is available to sign.

Signing Appointment...

At signing, you are going to review the settlement statement to ensure it makes sense and that the numbers there jive with what your loan officer has been telling you. If there are any questions or issues, then escrow will contact the loan person directly with questions. The escrow officer will have already told you prior to the signing appointment, what certified funds (if any) you will need to bring to your signing appointment and what form of photo identification they are going to need from you. Please make sure your identification is still valid. You do not want to be racing around to the DMV and trying to renew your expired driver's license during the mad rush to your closing date. Typical funds that you may need to bring to your signing appointment are for closing costs, your down payment, or other fees that you and your loan person have previously discussed. You should be aware of the funds needed to close your transaction before your signing appointment. Escrow will let you know what that amount needs to be (your loan person will most likely have already informed you as well) and you will need to get a certified check from your bank, made out per the escrow company's instruction. Sometimes this can be a last minute fire drill, so be prepared!

In some cases, all of the closing costs and pre-paid items have been covered either by the requested seller paid concessions (via your financing addendum) and/or by your earnest money deposit. At signing, you will see on the settlement statement where your earnest money deposit appears as a line item and you will note how it applies. You and your loan person will have discussed this. Your earnest money deposit could be going toward your purchase price, the down payment, or your closing costs. In some cases, you might even get your earnest money deposit refunded if it is not needed for any of those items. If that is your case, escrow will ask you at your signing appointment how you want that money refunded, a check or direct wire into your bank account? And they will let you know when that refund will be issued.

When you wrote up your offer, your agent hopefully asked you how you want to take title to the property. If you are single and buying

161

alone, then they enter your legal name and "*a single person.*" If you are a married couple then the agent puts in your legal names on the first page of the offer and writes in parentheses "*a married couple.*" If you are married but you are buying a property by yourself, your agent lists your name and enters "*a married person as her separate estate.*" If you are an unmarried couple buying together and you want the other person to automatically inherit your interest in the property should you pass away, then your agent enters your names and "*joint tenants in common with right of survivorship.*" If you are two friends buying together and you do not necessarily want the other person to inherit your interest in the property should you pass away, then your agent would write in "*joint tenants in common.*" These are some of the usual ways to take title and your agent can help speed things along by entering that on your offer paperwork. Otherwise, the escrow officer is going to ask how you want to take title or is going to confirm that what is written in the contract is in fact how you want title to be taken.

Once you have signed and the seller has completed their signing appointment, then escrow will bundle up all of your loan documents and courier them back to your loan person's underwriter. The underwriter will do a final review of all the documents. Once they are satisfied that all is good they will release the funds for your loan(s). Once escrow is notified that your loan has funded, they will make sure the deed is recorded with the county in your name. When the county records the deed in your name, then you are the new legal owner of the property. Escrow will then contact all parties to let them know the deal is now officially closed. At that point your agent can then go get the keys to the property for you. Never ask your agent if you can have the keys prior to closing. No sane listing or buyer's agent is going to provide keys to a buyer until they have been notified directly by escrow that your deal is closed and the deed is now recorded in your name.

No Access...

Prior to your closing date, please do not ask if you can store items in the vacant garage or have your new appliances installed in the kitchen. You do not own the property until it has recorded in your name. Therefore, you should never leave/store your personal items at the property or make any changes to that property until you are notified by escrow that you are the new owner. Even if the house is vacant, it is not yet yours. Prior to closing, what if you put your tools and some boxed items in the garage and they get stolen, or the garage burns down? Guess who is liable? The seller is liable. In your parents day these kinds of informal arrangements of storing items in a garage until closing were not so atypical. However, in today's litigious environment these arrangements should not happen. Another example of this, the house is empty, *"Does the seller mind if I go ahead and have the interior repainted prior to closing?"* Yes because there is liability on the seller's end and what if your deal does not close for some unforeseen reason? You have then paid to repaint a house you do not own. Prior to closing, please do not go over to the house and start pruning the bushes or cutting down the tree you do not like. It is tempting and you will be excited but please stay away. Avoid any temptation to do anything that could potentially get you in trouble. Wait until the place is legally yours.

Closing Plus Three...

In the old days it was not uncommon to have your closing date stated as, *"Closing plus three."* This meant the closing date was say March 31 and so you became the legal owner on the 31st but then you allowed the seller to remain in the property for three days after closing so they could move out. That is all but gone now. For good reason, i.e. the liability issues I just described and then some! There were many issues with what happens if the former owner damages the property during those three days, who is legally on the hook for repairs, what about injuries, etc.... There was usually no formal rental or lease agreement for those three days and thus the legal gray area was enormous. The law suits must have mounted regarding this issue because in Washington State that *"closing plus three"* option box was removed several years ago from the NWMLS purchase and sale agreement forms. A buyer most likely would not want to agree to *"closing plus three"* because why would he want a seller in his property for three days after closing? If for some reason a seller counters your offer by writing that verbiage in, I would advise rejecting it or have a real estate attorney review the pros and cons of that arrangement with you before you agree.

If for whatever reason the seller needs to do a leaseback option with you, i.e. they want to close on the property and then rent it back from you for a week or a month while they move out or they want to remain living there until their child's school year ends, then you absolutely want to have a local real estate attorney create a rental agreement for you to cover this. It should specify how damages will be handled, what kind of security deposit will be in play, who is going to hold that deposit in escrow, who is responsible for which utilities, and all the other items a normal apartment rental contract covers. Additionally, you would need to get information on landlord insurance and liability issues since you are not only the owner of the property but are now a landlord as well. Since you are then a landlord, what are your area's tenant/eviction laws? What if the seller refuses to vacate when their one month lease is up? Legally, your real estate agent and the listing agent should have no part in drafting this lease contract or in negotiating its terms and conditions.

Closing Day...

Your closing day will be clearly stated in your purchase and sale agreement. This is the date that the parties are agreeing title and ownership of the property will be transferred and recorded. Your closing day will never be on a legal holiday or a Saturday or Sunday. Please make sure you never plan on moving into your new place on the closing day. Sometimes your closing date has to be extended because your lender needs more time to close the loan. To extend the closing date, both parties must first agree to this in writing. In rare cases, a title condition hereto unknown may be discovered literally on closing day and cause the closing to be delayed. Also, the contract usually states the sellers are allowed to occupy the property until 9 p.m. of the closing day. If the deed records in your name at 2 p.m., your agent hands off the keys to you at 4 p.m., and you pull up in the drive way at 4:45 p.m. and the sellers are still there, you will know not to freak out. They are allowed to be there until 9 p.m. At 9:01 p.m. if the sellers are still there, then you can call the cops and create a big scene but technically not until then. Usually the sellers will have already moved out, the house will be vacant. But bear in mind the seller may move out on closing day and so they need space and time to get that taken care of.

For these reasons, I always advise that my buyers do not plan on moving in the new place until at least a week after the agreed upon closing date, longer if possible. If all goes well and the deal closes on time without issues, then you have a vacant house that you can start painting or fixing up prior to moving your stuff in. You will have some breathing room to get the new place set up and move out of your current place, clean your current place, etc....

Remember, that your first mortgage payment is not due until one month after you take possession. Sounds like a free month but that is not really the case and your loan person can explain this to you in greater detail. But from your checkbook's standpoint, you will not be making a mortgage payment that first month. That is great as you usually still have rent to pay for your old place and all the moving and other related expenses that come up when you move. So please give yourself as much time as possible to move out from your old place and into your new home. Whenever possible, try and avoid any rushed timelines, or tight holiday, and school related schedules. If you can plan ahead and give yourself more time, your nerves (and sore body) will thank you!

Real Life...

A while back, a friend of mine in another state had a friend who purchased a house. I referred some good agents I know in the area to this friend of a friend but she decided to work with an agent her co-worker used and raved about. Her deal was signed around and she and her agent showed up for her inspection. The inspector did not find any real issues, so all was looking good. Towards the very end of the inspection, her real estate agent gave the house keys to the inspector and asked him to lock up for her. He agreed and off she went.

The only person who is supposed to hold the keys and place them in or remove them from the key box is a licensed real estate agent or a licensed appraiser who has key box access. A home inspector is not someone who typically has a Supra, electronic key box pass and is authorized to operate it, nor are they supposed to be handling any keys to the property. Why the inspector agreed to do this is beyond me, much less why her agent did this! Anyway, the buyer took the keys from the inspector and said she would put them back in the key box for him. Once the inspector left, the buyer walked over to the nearby hardware store and had copies of the keys to the house made. The copies she kept and the original keys she put back in the key box and secured it.

A few days later, the buyer decided she wanted to measure the rooms in her soon to be home (she should have done this during her inspection). So she went over to the house and unlocked it, using her illegal set of keys. While she was inside, the next door neighbor called

167

the police and said someone who did not belong in the house was inside. The cops showed up and walked in on the buyer with guns drawn. When the seller was reached by the police, he told them he was the owner of the house and that he had not authorized anyone to be in his house and that no extra keys, besides the ones his listing agent had and the key box contained should be out there. The police called the listing agent who confirmed what the seller told them. The buyer was then arrested and charged with illegal entry and illegal possession of keys.

The last I heard, the deal went south in a hurry and now everyone is in litigation. The buyer's agent most likely will have her real estate license and her MLS membership suspended and face steep fines as she broke all kinds of rules and the law when she handed off the house keys to the inspector and left the property without securing the house and returning the keys to the key box. The buyer is being sued by the seller for illegally copying (stealing) the house keys and illegally entering the property. The seller is also suing the buyer's agent and her brokerage. The buyer is suing her agent and her brokerage. The inspector was reported and he is suing the buyer's brokerage and the buyer's agent.

Such fun! All of this happened because the buyer's agent did not follow very basic rules. It may seem like nothing to ask someone to put keys away for you, but look what can happen. Hopefully this story shows you that I am not kidding when I say keys should not be given out early, do not ask for them and please do not covertly copy them. For your own benefit, please do not go back to the property you are buying and wander around, try and gain unapproved access to it, make changes to it, drop items off, etc..., until escrow notifies you that the deed has recorded in your name and you are now the new legal owner.

EIGHT

LOOSE ENDS

Typical Players...

Let's sum up who the typical key players are in the home buying process.

1. <u>Buyer's Agent or Selling Agent</u>: The real estate agent who represents the buyer in the purchase of a property.

2. <u>Listing Agent</u>: The real estate agent who represents the seller in the sale of a property.

3. <u>Lender</u>: The institution or person who is loaning money to the buyer to purchase the home.

4. <u>Inspector</u>: The person the buyer selects and pays to inspect the property he is purchasing.

5. <u>Appraiser</u>: The person the lender's company contacts to go out and evaluate the subject property; i.e. make sure the loan is for a legitimate property and the sale price is of fair market value. The buyer pays for this, and the loan person will instruct when and how this payment is made. Note, loan officers are no longer allowed to cherry pick their appraisers. Appraisers are now randomly assigned to each property evaluation project.

6. <u>Title Company</u>: Usually selected by the seller when the property is first listed. They investigate the title for the subject property and make sure the title is clear and can be conveyed. The seller usually pays for this service.

7. <u>Escrow Company</u>: Buyer typically chooses this one. They are the third party referee who makes sure all money is disbursed properly and conditions to the purchase and sale agreement have been met. They ensure the deed is recorded by the county in the buyer's name. They notify all parties once the deed records and this is when the keys can be exchanged. The buyer and seller both pay for this service and it appears as a line item on your settlement statement. Note, sometimes (via your deal) the seller agrees to pay for your portion of the cost for this service.

There can be other entities involved but the above list is a good outline of who is usually involved in the home buying process.

A Good Agent...

Here is a list of what I think a good Buyer's Agent is going to do.

1. Always puts your best interest first.

2. Insists that you do an inspection on the property you are buying via the Inspection Contingency Form 35 (in WA State) or if a multiple offer scenario, tries to arrange for you to do a pre-inspection before you make an offer.

3. Has you sign the Inspector Referral Disclosure Form 41-D (in WA State) before you write up an offer which states any home inspector your agent has ever personally hired or is related to.

4. Remains at the property from the start until the very end of your inspection, secures the property and returns all keys to the key box.

5. Educates you about the home buying process prior to starting your search.

6. Provides you with a sample purchase and sale agreement to review prior to touring, so you can become familiar with it, ask any questions in advance.

7. Does not always tell you what you want to hear.

8. Refers you to a local real estate attorney (has a list for you to choose from) at any point during the purchase process if legal advice or help is needed.

9. Does not pretend to know everything and will say, "*I don't know the answer, let me look into that and get back to you.*" If it is a question of a legal nature, your agent cannot answer it even if he knows for sure what the answer is. Hopefully in that case, he will do what item eight states.

10. Respects your price cap and does not try and show you properties above that price point unless you ask.

11. Refers all loan questions, finance matters to your loan person.

12. Writes a custom cover letter that goes with your offer for the seller to review. This is especially important as most sellers today no longer want to meet your agent in person and have them present your offer directly to them. Rather, most sellers now prefer to have their agent get a copy of

your offer and then they sit down with their agent, either in person or now days sometimes online and over the phone and review your offer. The cover letter should give basic information about you, outline the main highlights of your offer, and provide contact information for your agent as well as your loan person. You should review this letter and make changes to it if you wish. As discussed, if it is a multiple offer situation, your agent may also have you write a personal letter to the seller as well. I can tell you that most buyer agents skip this cover letter step. Many times I have had feedback from a listing agent thanking me for including a cover letter and letting me know it impressed the seller and in some cases it has tipped the scales in my client's favor.

13. Ensures you get a complete copy of all paperwork, including everything you sign, either via email (with your permission) and/or hardcopy. You should receive copies of each form as you go, so you have it available, not get one big packet of all your paperwork on the day you close.

14. Does not guarantee that the property you are buying is going to make you money in the future or guarantees any current or future conditions concerning the property.

15. Does not profess to be the neighborhood expert, know everything about an area. He may know a lot and may even live in the area but he should not put himself out there as your primary source for information on a particular area.

Legally, you need to investigate each neighborhood/area independently and verify any zoning, environmental, construction feasibility, city public works projects, school changes, etc…, yourself and to your satisfaction. Your agent can help you find the right agencies/authorities to question but legally he should not be answering for those entities or relaying messages from them to you.

16. Follows Federal Fair Housing Law and does not tell you, *"That is a bad neighborhood, you don't want to live there."* as that is against the law. He can encourage you to review the neighborhood yourself, collect data on the area, talk to the local Community Patrol Officer, etc.…

17. Puts in writing that she does not give or receive compensation for referrals; i.e. lenders, inspectors, service people. Collecting certain referral fees is illegal (it is illegal for an agent and a loan person to give one another any kind of consideration for a client referral). If a referral fee is not illegal, you most likely still do not want your agent collecting or giving referral fees to line her pocket or influence her referral selections.

18. Helps you weigh the various pros and cons of the properties you are looking at.

19. Does not do dual agency deals, only represents you the buyer.

20. Does not poach other agents' clients; i.e. bad mouth other agents (either out right or in subtle passive aggressive ways)

and does not try to get other agents' clients to convert and work with them.

21. Remains grounded and helps you calm down if you become emotional.

22. Works with only one buyer per price range/criteria.

23. Is organized, timely and polite.

24. Checks in with you at least once a week, even once your deal is in the hands of your loan person and you are in the countdown to closing phase.

25. Maintains good records and paper trails all important communications involved in your transaction. You may see this as cc's on emails to other players in your deal or as an email that summarizes an earlier phone conversation.

A Good Buyer...

In fairness, a buyer needs to be aware of how their behavior affects the home buying process. Here is a list of traits a good buyer usually has.

1. Takes time up front to learn about the home buying process and organize things prior to looking.

2. Gets pre-approved for a loan and determines their price cap based on their budget.

3. Commits to working with one agent via a Buyer Agency Agreement so everyone is clear and all terms are stated up front. Remember, this does not mean you are stuck with that agent; the BAA should be revocable by either party at any time.

4. Provides their agent with a photo i.d. when they first meet, so the agent can copy that and turn it into his brokerage per their specific safety policies. Far too many agents (males included) are assaulted, even murdered each year while they are out in the field working. Asking for a valid photo i.d. from you is one way the industry is working to help mitigate this. This is not an insult, many of these violent acts against agents occur in the top tier markets by psychopaths who appear upscale and put together. Any agent who just throws you in a car or meets you at a property without first getting to know you, copying your i.d. is being reckless in terms of their own safety. You as a good buyer should respect this and not request or expect an agent blindly meet you at a property or take you out to look without having first given them your photo i.d. and taking time to meet in public and review working together.

5. Reads any information their agent suggests they review and asks any questions they may have.

6. Independently investigates any information/topics that could be an issue; i.e. zoning, schools, remodeling.

7. Takes responsibility for their purchase and the inherent risks and rewards.

8. Listens to their agent's instructions, and any posted listing agent instructions when touring a property.

9. Is respectful of others' property when touring.

10. When encountering other buyers and agents while touring, is polite and does not engage in talk about the subject property the sellers or what they are looking for, etc....

11. Does not blame their agent if they are not finding a property that meets all of their needs and wants. If you are receiving all the active listings per your search criteria, your agent does not have a magic wand to make your dream place appear.

12. Is not rigid in their criteria, and is able to review and possibly change their criteria based on the reality of the current market.

13. Does not ask their agent if a particular neighborhood or area is *"good or safe"* and does not ask their agent to set up their home search based on religious criteria; i.e. *"I need to be within eight blocks of the Synagogue."* It is against Federal Fair Housing Law for an agent to do either of those things. It is also unlawful for an agent to answer any questions regarding the racial, political, religious, demographic make-up of an area. Agents can and do get fined or lose their licenses in these situations via undercover Fair Housing shoppers, known as testers.

14. Does not lie or provide false information to their agent, loan person, title or escrow officer.

15. Reports anyone who asks them to falsify information or who they suspect are committing fraud to local professional boards and state oversight agencies.

16. Does not ask their agent to provide legal or tax advice or expect their agent to violate any licensing laws on their behalf.

17. Does not try and have their agent include personal property items in their purchase and sale paperwork and does not ask the agent to broker the sale or conveyance of personal items between the seller and buyer as a side transaction.

18. Does not ask their agent to make additional special trips and let them in the house they are buying before closing, i.e. to measure rooms, show their mother in-law, see what paint samples look like in different rooms, etc.... You should take care of those things during your inspection appointment or your final walk through. In some cases, sellers are not going to permit you to revisit except for the dates and times you are permitted to do so via your purchase and sale agreement.

19. Is aware their agent has other clients who also require time, have scheduled appointments and does not expect their agent to drop everything to accommodate them.

20. Does not use social media to bad mouth the seller or the property; i.e. boast about what a great deal they just got and how dumb the sellers are, especially prior to closing. I advise my buyers to keep their mouths shut, and their social media addictions at bay until the deal has closed and the keys are in their hands. Deals have literally imploded over a

buyer or seller posting information about each other/the deal online.

21. Keeps their agent informed at all times until the deal closes of any day trips, out of town work/vacation commitments, etc.... Makes sure their agent knows how to reach them at all times until their deal is closed.

Buyer's Remorse...

Most everyone has heard of buyer's remorse or experienced it firsthand when they have bought something only to determine after the fact they do not like it or it does not live up to all it was said to be. Hopefully, by getting organized up front and following the suggestions in this book you will avoid buyer's remorse. Certainly the more thought and organization you put into a home purchase, the better your end result should be. Still, once you have made an offer that is accepted and you are in a deal, you may get a case of the *"what ifs."* Also, like a swarm of locusts, everyone you know and their cousin Betty are going to come out of the woodwork and offer their opinion on what you are purchasing. Please do not let these Monday morning real estate quarterbacks negatively influence you. What's that expression, *"opinions are like...?"* You will know you have done your prep work by reading this book and other research. You will know that you took the time to pick the best people available to work with. This is not something you did impulsively or without research. Turn the peanut gallery off! It amazes me how almost everyone you meet or know will offer you an unsolicited opinion on real estate. There are also those who are jealous or have some other kind of problem and who seem to thrive on casting doubt about your home purchase or the way you are going about your real estate search. Most of these folks have watched way too much "reality" real estate TV shows. Please do not for a second believe those TV shows adequately show you what the home buying experience is like.

Blame Game, Victim...

I am astounded by the number of buyers that for years after their purchase will blame their agent for the choice they made. Just last week I had lunch with a friend and he had another person join us that I do not know. This woman found out I sell real estate and instantly launched into her home buying woes and what a horrible agent she had when she bought a couple of years ago. I do not know her agent but from what she relayed, the house she purchased sounds like a good deal especially for the limited budget she was working with and the area she wanted to buy in. I did not hear anything to indicate that her agent was slimy or misled her. But in this woman's mind everything she does not like about her house is her agent's fault. She blames the agent because her house does not have a fireplace. That was on her wish list but none of the houses she could afford had fireplaces. And that would be her agent's fault, because? She also blames her agent because her back yard slopes a certain way. She did not take note of this when touring, when doing her inspection and her agent is to blame for the slope of her back yard, really?

Another time I heard from someone at a party that their agent "made" them buy their house and now thanks to the crash in the economy his house is no longer worth what he paid for it. It is his agent's fault that he bought and the value went down, seriously? Must be a really persuasive and all knowing agent to have such power to "make" him buy and to have the the ability to know in advance the economy is going to crash and send home values downward for a while. Makes a lot of sense right? What agent wouldn't want their client to purchase a home and have it drop in value? I say that sarcastically.

This unfortunately is par for the course for real estate agent stories that I hear at least every month or so. Many times it does not sound to me like the person telling the story had a bad or unethical agent. Rather, I think in some cases they are pissy people who want to blame someone else for their aggravations, their lack of money, happiness, etc…, and who better to project all of that on then the bad old real estate agent? Don't get me wrong, this profession is rife with sleaze balls and skanky agents. But there are also wonderful people who are real estate agents, who work hard, are honest and truly work in their client's best interest. So whining and blaming the real estate agent for things like no fireplace, the sloping yard or the economy tanking and values decreasing is in my opinion childish.

If you set up your search and are organized like this book has shown you, then you can expect a better result. Becoming an informed home buyer also means you need to accept responsibility for your actions and decisions. You need to be accountable and not blame others for the decisions you make or for not getting everything you think you deserve. You can go out and work with someone who is unethical, be an uninformed buyer and purchase something that is not really so great. As a consolation, you can then legitimately play the victim role and blame the shady agent for years to come. Or you can choose to be an informed buyer and work with honest people. There is still some risk involved whenever you purchase but at least you have done as much homework as you can to make an informed decision. You might not get everything you want or discover later on that you really prefer something else. But you are an informed and responsible buyer, not a perpetual, whining, victim.

Fraud...

If you suspect anyone you are working with in the home buying process of committing fraud or perhaps you think what they are doing is not so ethical or a bit shady, then you should consider reporting it. You should first question them directly about whatever it is you think is problematic or not above board. If you still are not satisfied you can then escalate things.

If you believe your agent is not working on the up and up, and you have questioned them but are still not okay, then you should contact their designated broker or the owner of their brokerage. See what they have to say. Next, you could visit a real estate attorney, contact the local board of Realtors (if your agent is a member of NAR), contact the state licensing department's real estate division and there is always the state attorney general's office.

If your loan person is doing something that you think is shady and their response to your concern is not acceptable, then you should contact their branch manager, the company's main office, then a real estate attorney, the state department that covers financial institutions and finally the state attorney general's office.

There are also the local media outlets with their consumer reporters, who are usually chomping at the bit to report a fraud story on a local entity. Just make sure you are not acting prematurely or flying off the handle and that what you are concerned about is legitimate. You need to have documentable evidence, not just *"he said/she said"* and you need to have given whomever you have a problem with ample time to respond to your query and concern.

Real Life...

Many years ago, I had a buyer who was purchasing her first home. She had been to one of my buyer classes, done all of her homework and was ready to make the move. We set up her search based on her criteria and began touring. She began asking somewhat odd questions about home values and why not purchase in another area. I could tell someone was feeding her questions, trying to make her doubt herself. I set up another search for her in the new area she had mentioned. There was a property in her new search area that was a nice house but one problem, it was literally right next to the freeway. The noise, the smog, the fact the freeway is never going to go away, all made that a bad investment choice in my mind, especially when she had much better options.

I also could not figure out why she had suddenly chosen this new area when the original neighborhood she had us looking in offered way better value and amenities for the same amount of money. After much stewing, she finally agreed that buying a house next to the freeway when she could afford (for the same price) something in a quieter and more desirable neighborhood did not make sense. Back to the original neighborhood we went for our tours.

Suddenly her "best friend" began to tour with her. They had known each other since high school and this "friend" hated me on sight. If I commented on how sunny it was outside, the "friend" would immediately say something like, *"That's not true, it's getting cloudy and it is going to rain."* She was a complete hostile nut. I let it slide. As we continued touring houses, I began to see that this "best friend" of my client was extremely jealous. My client was looking at houses in a neighborhood that was better than where the "best friend" owned. I also discovered this "friend" was a self proclaimed real estate expert who was giving my client horrific advice. It turns out the "friend" had an agent she wanted my client to work with and it was clear they were working overtime behind the scenes to get me canned. This agent is one of the well known glitzy agents who looks terrific to the uninformed public but within the industry is notorious for his less than ethical practices. I found out later there was a referral/conversion fee involved between this agent and the "best friend." This agent was paying the "best friend" to get my client to switch and work with him. How feculent! Long story short, my client listened to her "best friend" and decided to not work with me anymore. She terminated our buyer agency agreement and life moved on.

About a year later, this former would-be buyer client contacted me and apologized for ditching me. She told me that she appreciated the hard work I did for her and the advice I gave her and wished she had followed it. It turns out she purchased another house right next to the freeway (which was listed by guess who, the shark she ended up working with—i.e. dual agency). She hates the house's location and is no longer friends with her high school chum. She realized too late that her former "best friend" was not a true friend and was in reality a jealous and manipulative person.

Not all stories are like this or end this way. Sometimes you and your agent for whatever reason just do not work well together and decide to part ways. In this particular case all was not horrible for me, as this former would-be client has since referred two people to work with me. I can assure you that the two clients she referred did not buy houses next to the freeway and I did not sell to them in a dual agency capacity, nor did I pay her any money for the referrals. I would caution buyers to be aware of others' agendas when they are purchasing a home, be they best friends, family or otherwise. People you know and like can get very jealous and manipulative (consciously and unconsciously) when you are buying a house and they do not always truly have your best interest at heart. Do not become paranoid but try and keep your own agenda on track and do not allow others to muddy the waters with their own baggage and agendas.

Final Word...

I hope this book is informative and helps you in your home buying quest. I did not state you would finish this book and be a real estate expert, nor did I say that my way (my opinions) are the only way. The goal is you are better informed about the whole home buying process having read this book. You now have the background needed to ask crucial questions and to recognize a red flag when you see one. If you found this book helpful, please recommend it to others. The companion book, <u>Home</u> <u>Selling</u> <u>for</u> <u>Smarties</u> is available for anyone you know who is considering selling their home. If you need a laugh and a light read, my satirical real estate mystery novels are also available, the titles are listed in the "About the Author" section as is my contact information. Here's to being an informed home buyer and enjoying life, cheers!

NINE

QUICK GLANCE

This chapter provides you with a quick reference guide and a book review quiz.

You Are Here...

Here is an outline of the basic steps to buying a property. It does not include any deal specifics or common variations.

1. Select your agent and sign a Buyer's Agent Agreement.

2. Pick your loan person and get pre-approved for your loan.

3. Tour properties and choose one.

4. Make an offer, with it goes your earnest money deposit.

5. Offer accepted.

6. Contact your insurance company and make written application for your home insurance.

7. Hire your inspector(s) and pay them to inspect the property before your inspection contingency expires.

8. Complete your inspection period and continue moving forward with the deal.

9. Deliver your earnest money deposit check to the escrow company.

10. Your loan person orders the appraisal of the property; you pay for this as instructed by your loan person.

11. Review the title report and title updates that the title company sends to you regarding the property you are purchasing.

12. Attend your scheduled signing appointment with escrow. You will be signing your final loan paperwork and reviewing your estimated settlement statement and verifying the numbers on that statement match what your loan person has told you to expect.

13. Receive notification from escrow that the deed has recorded in your name and now you are the new property owner.

14. Get the keys to your new home and begin the moving process.

15. Thank your agent and loan person for helping you through this seemingly endless maze of obscure steps! If you truly like them, then refer them to your friends and family.

Loan Peeps...

Here is a basic list of the people who are involved in completing your loan and making sure your mortgage happens.

1. **Loan officer or mortgage broker**: the financial salesperson who you choose to work with, who assesses your financial situation and pre-approves you for a loan product to finance your property purchase. This is your primary money contact person throughout your home buying odyssey and they keep you updated as to your loan application's progress and walk you through the lender's maze to secure your mortgage.

2. **Processor**: the person assigned to work with your loan officer/mortgage broker who organizes your file's

paperwork and begins to execute the necessary steps to secure your loan.

3. **Appraiser**: the person who is contacted by the lender to complete the appraisal. The appraisal is the process by which the lender assesses the property you are purchasing and makes sure you are purchasing a viable property at a fair market price. You pay for this and your loan person will let you know how much it will cost and when to pay for it.

4. **Underwriter**: the person within your loan person or mortgage broker's company who reviews your loan file and your signed around purchase and sale agreement. They ensure there are no outstanding conditions or issues with you, your loan, or the property that you are using their company's money to buy. This is the person escrow sends your signed loan documents to for final review and approval. They notify escrow on the closing day that the funds for your loan have been released.

Review Quiz...

1. Susan and Mahesh are pre-approved buyers. They visit a new construction site and are interested in purchasing one of the units for sale. The site agent tells them he can write their offer up for them. What should they do?

2. Madeline receives a blank purchase and sale agreement from her real estate agent to review prior to touring houses. She has several specific legal questions about it and a tax

question. Is it okay for her agent to answer her legal questions? Is her agent the best person to answer tax questions?

3. Thomas and Tamara are purchasing a new construction townhouse. When they are writing up their offer, their real estate agent tells them it is a new construction property and they do not need to pay for an inspection. He advises they not include an inspection contingency with their offer. What should they do?

4. Maurice's lender tells him she will only work with him if he agrees to work with Amy from ABC Realty. What should Maurice do?

5. Shalimar's cousin, Ricardo, just got his real estate license and wants to be her agent. Her boss knows a real estate agent, Jan, and he is constantly asking Shalimar if she is working with Jan yet. What should Shalimar consider telling her cousin and boss?

6. Cynthia found a house she likes while looking online. Her agent tells her she should forget about it because it is in a bad neighborhood. What should Cynthia do?

7. Tuan is relocating from Chicago. He asks his agent if a house they have just toured is in a bad area. His agent tells him she cannot answer that question. He becomes annoyed and decides to find a new agent to work with who will answer all of his questions. Is this a wise choice on Tuan's part?

8. When is the best time for Judy and Jill to think about the earnest money deposit and make sure the funds are in their checking account?

9. Sherry is looking for a condo in Seattle. She decides she will have two agents work for her. One is from XYZ Realty and the other is from ABC Realty. Sherry thinks this will give her an advantage because two agents must be better than one. Also, since they are working for different companies they will be able to show her more properties. Is Sherry right?

10. When writing up an offer what are the two factors you as a buyer need to take into account when figuring out what your offer price is going to be?

11. Is the term "broker" something that should impress me?

Quiz Answers...

1. Susan and Mahesh should politely refuse. The site agent might be the most ethical and informed agent on the planet but most likely he is contracted to sit the site and represent the seller (developer) of the property. Thus, if he writes up the buyer's offer he could be acting as a dual agent. Susan and Mahesh need to have their own buyer's agent helping them and showing them new construction properties or other resale properties. It is important to note, sometimes new construction sites have a required registration roster for your first visit to the site. If you sign in on their roster and do not indicate that you are currently working with an

agent and provide the agent's name, brokerage name and contact information, then quite possibly the new construction site will require you have them write up your offer on a property in their development. Or they will state no commission, or a greatly reduced commission, will be paid to any other agent that represents you in an offer on one of their new construction properties. This is another reason why it is important for you to set up your team ahead of time and have a good buyer's agent working for you and assisting you with all of your tours. Sometimes, buyers who are not yet working with agents or even approved for a loan, wander into a new construction site, and innocently sign in on the required roster. Then after they see a new place they like, they go out and find an agent and secure financing. This would be backwards as the information above shows because their agent will likely not get paid for helping them with their purchase.

2. It is never okay for Madeline's real estate agent to answer her legal questions. All legal questions must be referred to a local real estate attorney. Her agent is also not the person to ask about tax related questions. Madeline should consult with a tax professional. Go to the appropriate sources to get the best information and results.

3. Thomas and Tamara should run! Fire any agent who tells you that you do not really need to do an inspection on the property you are interested in buying. Same with any new

construction site agent that insists you do not need to do an inspection since it is new and your lender most likely will not require you do an inspection and besides, the developer is providing you with a warranty. In my opinion, it is always in your best interest to have your offer contingent upon an inspection and pay to have one (or more) done. The exception mentioned is a multiple offer situation. In that case you should try and get the seller's permission to have a pre-inspection done on the property before you submit your offer.

4. Maurice should also run. This is a tie-in situation. In states where tie-in's are illegal (WA State is one) no one can require you to work with someone else as a condition for them agreeing to work with/represent you. So a loan person cannot say they will only do your loan if X real estate agent works with you or vice-versa.

5. Shalimar should politely tell everyone that this is business first, nothing personal. She will make up her own mind as to those she chooses to represent her/work with her. She is not going to be pressured or manipulated by others into working with people she does not first fully investigate and believe are a good match for her.

6. Cynthia should report this agent for violating the Federal Fair Housing Law. No real estate agent is permitted to tell you that an area is good or bad or not a place you would

want to live. You have to make that determination on your own.

7. This was not a wise choice on Tuan's part as his real estate agent was following Federal Fair Housing Law. Tuan needs to investigate all neighborhoods on his own and reach his own conclusions as to whether or not they are suitable for him.

8. Judy and Jill should have their earnest money deposit funds in their checking account before they start their home tour. A good agent is going to review this with them at their first intake meeting and help them plan accordingly.

9. Sherry is incorrect. You want to sign one Buyer's Agency Agreement with one real estate agent per metro region. For example, you would not sign a BAA with an agent who sells in the north part of town and another BAA with an agent who sells in the south part of town. Most buyer agents will cover both areas of town. An exception to this would be, you are considering living in the Seattle metro area and also considering living in Bellingham (a city about two hours north of Seattle). In this case, you could sign a BAA with an agent who works in Seattle and another BAA with an agent who works in Bellingham. You need to first inform both agents that you are doing this. Then each of the agents can show you what their city has to offer and you can make up your mind from there. Sherry is also incorrect in thinking that having two agents from two different

194

brokerages helping her will be an advantage. All agents who are members of the local MLS have the same access to new listings and properties. In the old days, prior to this business going mostly online, there were pocket listings and neighborhood specialists and buyers used to get more than one person to help them because it was true then that some agents had more access to listings before they were published in the MLS listing books and delivered to everyone. This is no longer the case and no brokerage has an "in" or corner on new listings or area specific listings anymore. Also, there are no more in-house bonuses for agents who sell one their own brokerage's listings versus another brokerage's listing. This is illegal now. So an agent from XYZ Realty who sells an XYZ Realty listing does not earn a penny more, via any bonus, than if he sells a listing from ABC Realty.

10. A buyer should take into consideration the statistical data (active and sold comps) regarding a property of interest and their intuitive feel for a property when they are writing up an offer.

11. The generic term "broker" should not impress you. In WA State, that term is used to refer to any person who has a real estate license. Regardless of where you live, remember to investigate titles, designations, and awards that any agent or loan person touts and find out firsthand exactly what they mean before you are blindly impressed.

GLOSSARY

(Written from a buyer's perspective)

ASHI: American Society of Home Inspectors.

Appraisal: the independent valuation of the property you are buying. This is ordered by your lender and is required for your loan. Appraisers are no longer cherry picked or assigned to lenders; it is now a lottery assignment system. The **Appraiser** is the licensed person who actually goes out in the field and evaluates the property you are buying. This typically happens after the removal of your inspection contingency. The buyer pays for the appraisal; your lender should let you know in advance the cost of this and terms of payment. Once your deal has closed, make sure you contact your lender and have them mail you a copy of your appraisal report; they will not always automatically do this. Keep the appraisal report on file as it can come in handy later; i.e. you need new gutters and want to know the exact exterior square footage around your house, that's in the appraisal report!

As Is: a term typically used to indicate the property is being sold in its current condition and the seller is not open to addressing any repairs a buyer may want taken care of prior to closing. It is a term that is sometimes mistakenly used to indicate that the seller assumes no legal responsibility for the condition of the property and/or the seller will not provide a seller disclosure statement, even when required by law.

Bank Owned: a term used to describe a property that has been foreclosed on and is now for sale by the lien holder, bank. These properties are notorious for not being well maintained.

Buyer Agency Agreement: (**BAA**) a written agreement whereby the buyer and agent spell out the terms of their working relationship. It includes the buyer's name, agent's name, agent brokerage's name, a start and end date, any geographical exclusions, and states the agreement is revocable by either party at any time when notification of termination is provided in writing.

CC&Rs: the Covenants, Conditions, and Regulations for a condominium or co-op. Usually this is delivered with the Resale Certificate or the Public Offering Statement for the buyer to review.

Cash Offer: an offer on a property that is made without a financing contingency or lender involved. The buyer intends to pay for the property using cash, not a loan.

Closing: the date you and the seller agree upon, via your purchase and sale agreement, to finalize the deal and convey title from the seller to the buyer and record the deed in your name. All purchase and sale agreements must have a clearly stated closing date in order to be valid and enforceable. Writing in "*to be determined*" in the closing date blank is not acceptable. Closing will not occur on a legal holiday, Saturday or Sunday.

Comparison Reports: the statistical reports for active and sold properties that are similar to the property you are interested in making an offer on. Any member of your local MLS should be able to run these reports for you prior to writing up an offer. Also referred to as a **CMA, Comparative Market Analysis** or **Comps**.

Condominium: a shared housing complex whereby you own your actual unit and have common shared areas that are jointly owned and maintained by the homeowner's association. There are monthly or annual homeowner dues and all owners must abide by the CC&Rs.

Co-op: (**cooperative**) a shared housing complex where you own stock (shares) in the controlling corporation that actually owns all of the units. Your shares in the corporation are usually determined via the square footage and floor level of your particular apartment. There are monthly or annual homeowner dues and all owners must abide by the CC&Rs. All sales of apartments must first be approved by the co-op board before interest can be assigned and shares issued. It is harder to obtain financing for a co-op as opposed to a condominium.

Counter Offer: when a named party makes a change to an offer or rejects it outright and creates a new offer. Example, the buyer offers $320,000 and the seller counter offers back for $330,000. Then the buyer counters the seller's counter offer at $325,000, etc....

Current State of the Market: a phrase used to describe the housing market's condition; i.e. is it a seller's market or a buyer's market? Are sales fast or slow? Usually it shows how things are trending overall in a region or area. Note, there are micro market conditions; i.e. a specific neighborhood or price point may be moving fast but the rest of the market is very slow and not selling.

Deed: the written document that conveys the title to real property from the seller to the buyer. Escrow makes sure the appropriate county records this document and then notifies all parties the deal is closed and keys can be given out.

Dual Agent: an agent who represents both the buyer and seller in the sale of a property and is paid both the selling and listing office commissions for doing so. This is illegal in some states and in other states you the buyer and the seller have to agree in writing first before this can occur.

Earnest Money Deposit: (EMD) the amount of money the buyer pledges when making an offer to let the seller know you are serious about following through on your offer. This is usually tendered via a hard copy check or by an **Earnest Money Promissory Note** (a legally binding instrument that essentially substitutes for a check) when making your offer.

Easement: the right usually noted in your title report which gives, for example, the utility company permission to access the subject property to maintain their equipment, power lines, water pipes, etc.... Another common example is where the common driveway that crosses the subject property is noted and it is fully accessible to all parties which use it for ingress and egress to their adjoining properties. There are many forms of easements (implied, in gross, necessity) you can research or ask your title representative about these.

Escalation Addendum: an addendum to a buyer's offer that spells out how much over the offered price the buyer is willing to go in order to beat any competing offers. Usually escalation increments start at $1,000 and are used in multiple offer situations.

Escrow: the process where something of value is held by a neutral third party until contractual conditions have been met. This would be your earnest money deposit being held by the **Escrow Agent** (the escrow company) and later disbursed per the terms of your purchase and sale agreement and your loan officer's instructions. The escrow agent is selected when you are negotiating your offer. The **Escrow Officer** is a licensed person who works for the escrow agent (company). The escrow officer prepares your settlement statement per your lender's and the purchase and sale agreement's instructions and ensures all money is paid and applied where indicated. Escrow ensures once your funds are released by your lender, that the title is conveyed, and the deed is recorded in your name. Escrow notifies all parties once the deed is recorded in the buyer's name. The escrow fee is usually split equally between the seller and buyer but sometimes the buyer negotiates the seller paying his half of the escrow fee.

Equity: the value you have in your property above the amount you owe on the property. Example, if your mortgage amount is $150,000 and your property's current market value (what you can get selling it today) is $320,000, then your equity is $170,000 (less selling fees and taxes). **Negative Equity,** is the economists polite way of saying you are losing money; i.e. your loan amount is $150,000 and your property's current market value is $100,000, thus you are $50,000 in the red.

Fair Market Value: the price or value that a specific property is worth based on market conditions at that point in time. Sometimes described as **what the market will bear,** the **market rate,** or the **going price.**

Financing Addendum: the part of a buyer's offer that outlines the buyer's specific loan conditions and timelines necessary for the buyer to secure their financing and complete the purchase.

Flipping: a term used when someone purchases a property that is in need of cosmetic upgrades and repair and they quickly fix it up in hopes of reselling it at a higher price and for a profit.

Foreclosure: when a lien holder (bank) evicts the mortgagor (home owner) who has defaulted on their home loan and takes back possession of the property. They usually then sell it in order to fully or partially satisfy the lien (loan). Foreclosed properties are also referred to as **bank owned.**

Full Service Agent: a traditional full time real estate agent who works with his clients from the very start of their home buying process all the way until closing and then follows up for years thereafter. He usually does not charge the buyer for any services rendered during the home buying process. This is in contrast to other business models where the buyer is passed off to different people during the home buying process, the agent only works part time, or the buyer pays flat rate fees for various services provided to assist them in the home buying process.

Home Buyer Warranty: a form of insurance or warranty a buyer or seller may purchase to cover stated items/systems in the subject property for a certain period of time after a transaction closes. Most usually cover the basic systems in a house; the furnace, appliances.

Home Owners Association: a group of home owners with a common or shared interest in a condominium, co-op or neighborhood. Members usually must pay monthly or annual monetary dues and are allotted voting powers for common projects and special assessments. The association usually elects a board to help manage the association and run things.

Home Owners Insurance: insurance a buyer pays for to cover the specific property he is buying. For a house, it will cover the house itself and the lot it sits on. For a condominium, it will cover the inside of the unit itself and usually a separate storage unit if applicable. Lenders require buyers purchase this, as do condominium home owner associations. Those purchasing a single family house with cash are strongly encouraged to purchase this form of insurance too.

Inspection Contingency: the clause or form that makes a buyer's offer contingent upon a specified inspection time period, typically a week after the mutual acceptance date. During this time, a buyer may personally inspect the property and/or hire professional inspectors to look at it as well.

Law of Real Estate Agency: a pamphlet that is required in WA State to be given to all buyers and sellers of real estate. It describes a consumer's legal rights when dealing with a real estate broker in WA State.

Legal Description: the description of the property you are purchasing stated in legal terms. This verbiage is provided by the title company and in some states is required to be mutually acknowledged by both parties and included in the purchase and sale agreement paperwork in order for mutual acceptance to occur.

Lead Disclosure: a Federal booklet which explains the dangers of lead based paints and how this comes into play when buying a property. It is mandatory that this booklet be given to all home buyers and sellers. If a property was built prior to 1978 (the year lead in paint was banned in the United States), then a lead disclosure addendum needs to be included when writing up an offer and acknowledged by the seller, listing agent, the buyer, and the buyer's agent.

MLS: the Multiple Listing Service. This is the most common listing service in the United States that the majority of real estate agents belong to. It is membership based, meaning agents pay annual dues to be a member to their local affiliate and they must abide by member rules and regulations as stipulated by the MLS. The MLS is a vast, organized database of local or regional listings. The MLS is where most agents post their listings and buyer's agents go to search for available listings and check a property's status. The MLS is where most independent real estate websites around the country pull listings from to post on their sites. Each state or region within a state typically has its own MLS or listing organization. For example, in western Washington State it is the Northwest Multiple Listing Service (**NWMLS**).

Mortgagee: the party that lends the buyer money to purchase a property (the lending institution).

Mortgagor: the party that takes out the loan to purchase a property (the buyer).

Multiple Offers: when a property for sale is soliciting or has more than one offer being made on it at one time. A specific date and time are usually given for offer submissions in a multiple offer situation. A buyer should attempt to do a pre-inspection on the property if they are going to waive their inspection contingency as part of their multiple offer strategy. Usually you include an escalation addendum or sometimes the seller states they only want your best offer, no escalation addendums.

Mutual Acceptance: the term used to describe when a buyer and seller have come to a complete or a mutual meeting of the minds and all of the terms of a deal are agreed upon. This is also referred to as **Mutual Agreement**. This is when your offer has been fully accepted by the seller and from this point the timelines in your purchase and sale agreement activate and the clock starts ticking.

NAR: the National Association of Realtors, founded in 1908. Real estate agents who are members are called Realtors (a trademarked term) and are bound by the organization's Code of Ethics.

Neighborhood Review: the time period a buyer has to review a neighborhood or area where she is purchasing a home. A wise buyer is going to do their own independent review of a neighborhood prior to writing up an offer. The Inspection Contingency Form 35 (WA State) allows for a buyer to request a neighborhood review and then usually have three days after mutual acceptance is reached to review the neighborhood and terminate the transaction should they not like what they find.

Personal Property: items that are not permanently attached to the land or house. Examples: bird bath, freestanding bookshelf units, sofa, washing machine (if not noted as an appliance that stays in the listing report). The seller takes these items with him when he moves, unless there is a separate written agreement between the buyer and the seller regarding these types of items (which agents legally should not assist with or be a part of).

Pre-Approval: a certificate or letter provided by a buyer's lender which states that a buyer has been approved for a loan (mortgage). It usually states the buyer's name, purchase price, loan amount, loan to value ratio, loan type(s), the term of the loan (i.e. 20 years), funds needed to close, any special conditions, the loan person's name and company name. The purchase price indicated on the initial pre-approval form is not always the amount a buyer wants to spend. It merely shows the maximum amount a buyer can spend based on his loan pre-approval. A buyer's pre-approval certificate or letter should always be updated to reflect the specific monetary conditions and amounts in her offer. It is usually valid for a few months after it is issued. It is not a commitment to lend but it does show that a buyer has met with the loan person and they have most likely run credit, reviewed numbers, talked about various loans that are available and verified certain lending conditions are met. A wise buyer's agent is going to request a copy of this pre-approval from a buyer before starting to work with them.

Public Offering Statement: (**POS**) the document that a new construction condominium project provides a buyer within a specified number of days after mutual agreement which outlines the organization and structure of the new or soon to be formed home owner's association. It shows the estimates for home owner's dues and collection schedules, projected budgets for operations and management, reserves, etc.... Usually the CC&Rs are delivered with this document. In WA State, a buyer has seven days after receipt to review the POS, ask questions and/or terminate the deal based on this review.

Purchase and Sale Agreement: (**PSA**) the documents that are used to create your offer on a property. The PSA is the enforceable agreement or contract that the buyer and the seller have both fully acknowledged. It details the terms, conditions and timelines the buyer and the seller are working under for the sale of the property. This can also be referred to as your **Agreement, Contract, Deal, Transaction.**

Real Estate Agent: a term used to describe anyone who is licensed to sell real estate. Also commonly referred to as an **Agent**, **Salesperson**, **Broker**.

Real Property: a term used to describe the land and/or anything permanently attached to it. Example, a lot with a ranch style house built on it or a lot with a condominium complex built on it.

Realtor: a person who is licensed to sell real estate and is also a member of the National Association of Realtors. The Association trademarked this term in 1949. Pronounced "real"+ "tor"—there is no "i" in the middle.

Resale Certificate: the document a buyer receives when purchasing an existing (not new construction) condominium or co-op. It usually states the monthly dues, gives ownership ratios, financial reserves, notes any special assessments, and indicates if there is pending litigation against the homeowner's association. The CC&Rs are usually delivered with this certificate for the buyer to review. In WA State, a buyer has five days after receipt to review the Resale Certificate, ask questions and/or terminate the deal based on this review. This is also sometimes called the **Resale**.

Rescission: the termination of a deal by both of the parties involved. Usually acknowledged by both parties in writing via a specific form depending on the legal reason the parties are terminating the deal.

Seller Disclosure Statement: the form that is required in some states for sellers to fill out and provide to a buyer that states certain known conditions or knowledge a seller may have about the property they are selling. In the NWMLS this form is commonly called the **Form 17**.

Settlement Statement: the final tally sheet that escrow puts together outlining all credits and debits for the buyer and seller and disbursements. As a buyer, you will only see your side of this tally and will want to verify the numbers are accurate. The review of this statement occurs at your signing appointment. Once fully executed, this statement is also sometimes referred to as the **Final HUD**.

Short Sale: when the owner of a property does not have enough money to pay off their existing mortgage upon the sale of their property. The shortage of funds has to be negotiated by the seller and the lender (mortgage note holder).

Signing Appointment: the appointment you will attend to review your final loan paperwork and to sign off on it. You also get and review your settlement statement at this appointment. This appointment is set up by escrow and they will let you know what form of photo identification and any funds you need to bring with you. In escrow states (WA State), your signing appointment is separate from the seller's signing appointment and there usually are a few days after signing until closing takes place. In traditional settlement states, you have a concurrent signing appointment with the seller and the deal closes the same day.

Title: the legal ownership of real property. Usually it is indicated by the filed written document called the deed.

Title Insurance: protects against future losses occurring as a result of past events. The seller pays for the title company to guarantee clear title for the property they are selling. A lender typically requires a buyer pay for a title insurance premium so as to protect their interest in the property they are loaning money on to purchase. Cash buyers are encouraged to purchase this insurance as an owner's policy.

Title Report: a document compiled by the chosen title company which details the condition of the title to a specific piece of property. A preliminary title report is usually pulled when a listing agent first takes a listing. Once a deal is signed around, the title company works on any title related issues and updates the title report as is necessary until the deal closes.

CHARLES CHAPLIN

ABOUT THE AUTHOR

Charles Chaplin is a Managing Broker and was originally licensed in 1991 in Washington, DC. Charles has been selling real estate in the greater Seattle metro area since 1997. Since 2004, Charles has volunteered to teach hundreds of state certified home buyer classes. He is a certified clock hour instructor and a certified state bond program instructor. Charles is a multi-year Five Star Agent Award winner for *Seattle Magazine* and *Portland Monthly*. He has a B.A. in Economics and Communications.

If you need help with buying or selling a home in the greater Seattle metro area, or you need an agent referral for your part of the country, or you are an agent who would like information to join Charles' agent referral network, please reference this book's title in the subject header and send an email to Charles@lifeinseattle.com.